The Great Cars

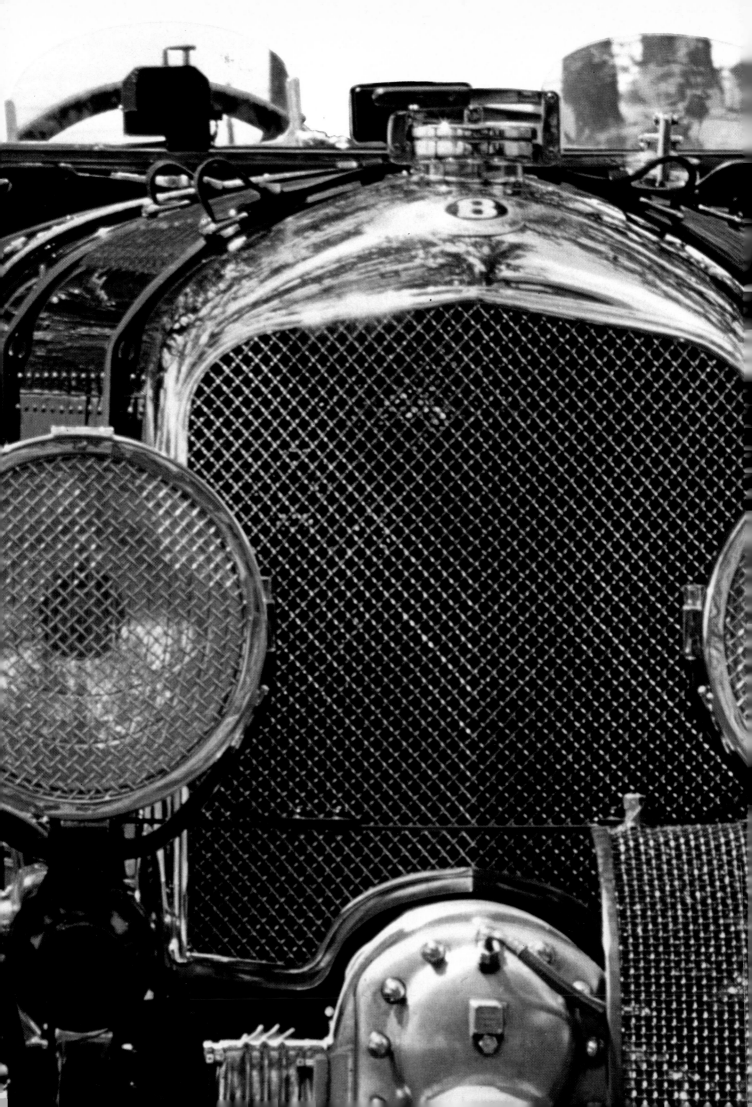

A Ridge Press Book
Grosset & Dunlap/New York

The Great Cars *by* Ralph Stein

Special Photography by Tom Burnside

Editor-in-Chief: Jerry Mason
Editor: Adolph Suehsdorf
Art Director: Albert Squillace
Art Associate: Allan Mogel
Art Associate: David Namias
Associate Editor: Moira Duggan
Associate Editor: Frances Foley
Art Production: Doris Mullane

---

*All rights reserved,
including the right of
reproduction in whole or in part
Prepared and produced by
The Ridge Press, Inc.
Published by Grosset & Dunlap, Inc.,
New York, N. Y.
Published simultaneously in Canada
Library of Congress
Catalog Card Number 67-21149
Printed by
Mondadori Editore, Italy*

Contents

What Made Them Great 6

INVICTA 20 *Talbot-Lago* 26

Lanchester 34

Hispano-Suiza 44 *Alfa Romeo* 54

vauxhall 70 Rolls-Royce 78 BENTLEY 96

DUESENBERG 106 Frazer Nash 114

CORD 122 MERCEDES-BENZ 128

ferrari 142 Simplex 150 BUGATTI 158

MERCER 176 M.G. 184

Jaguar 196 STUTZ 206 Delage 212

LINCOLN 220

Isotta-Fraschini 224 PACKARD 230

LANCIA 238

ASTON MARTIN 244

Index 251

What Made Them Great

When I sat down to write about the great cars, I knew that I had set myself a difficult task. But I did not foresee quite how hard it would turn out to be. I had room for twenty-five cars. But which twenty-five? For surely more cars than that deserve to be called great. Being lazy, I first chose those which I knew best from personal experience. This category alone almost filled my allotted space, for it always has been easy to write most about those I love most. Next I included cars that have long fascinated me, even though I have had little actual experience with them—the Lanchester, for example. By then I had used up all my pages. I should have liked to have written about the early Renaults, Napier, Panhard, Cadillac, the Model T Ford, the White and Stanley Steamers, Locomobile, Lozier, Delahaye; I even wanted to include that great American automobile, the Welch, mostly because I've lived with one for many years and intimately know its foibles, its virtues, and its odd felicities of design. And even including all of these I would have neglected some great makes.

But I submit that the cars in this book are among the greatest of many great cars.

This is the place to remember all those individuals and organizations which have furthered this work.

I thank Henry Austin Clark, Jr., Ralph Buckley, Zora Arkus-Duntov, Ed Bond, George Schieffelin, the AMA Library in Detroit, the builders of many of the cars mentioned and their helpful publicity people, Harrah's Automobile Collection in Reno, Nevada, and The Autocar *and* Old Motor *in London.*

Tom Burnside could not have made his incomparable color photographs of the cars without the enthusiastic help of their owners. To them sincere thanks, too.

R.S.

"Tumbrils End"
Westbrook, Connecticut

What Made Them Great

Great cars have one thing in common: from the nineteenth-century Panhard to the latest Ferrari they all feel alive when you drive them. They have a vitality of their own which you can feel transmitted to your hands and feet through their steering wheels, their pedals, their shift levers. Ettore Bugatti knew this and used the words *le pur sang* and a drawing of a wild-maned, pure-blooded horse on his catalogues. Enzo Ferrari uses a horse, too. Marc Birkigt flaunted a flying stork on the radiator cap of his Hispano-Suiza. (I must admit, however, that some recent felines and Indian ponies are mere adornment.)

In the beginning only the rare, perceptive motorist understood that he was driving a better-than-usual motorcar, for the early autoist was generally a rotten driver. He was a nineteenth-century man and you couldn't really expect him suddenly to deal with machines which could blast along at a fearful twenty-five miles an hour and which, to him, were devilishly complex to boot.

The most intricate mechanisms that the driver of 1900 had any experience with were the steam locomotive and his wife's sewing machine. And it was hardly likely that he ever ran either of these. True, he owned a watch, but he had no more intimate knowledge of its mysteries than you have of the one on your wrist this minute. No wonder then that when he abandoned his bicycle or his horse-drawn buggy and found himself, terrified, at the controls of an automobile he just couldn't cope.

Shifting gears without making frightful graunching noises or stalling the engine was a nightmare. (He had but a hazy idea of what those wheels with teeth were all about, anyhow.) He was baffled by any slight indisposition of the mechanism which might keep his car from starting, or cause it to expire, suddenly and mystifyingly, on the road. His usual remedy was a farmer's horses.

Sometimes he even had no more than a vague notion of the difference between oil and gasoline. There is a pitiful account of just such nineteenth-century ignorance in a 1902 treatise on automobiles, "Motors and Motor Driving," edited by Sir Alfred Harmsworth. The sad tale quotes the motoring diary of a Mr. and Mrs. Koosens.

Mr. Koosens says: "Early in 1895, while travelling in Germany, I saw an advertisement of a motor-car builder with an illustration of a car. My wife said she liked the look of the thing, so I ordered one. I had then never seen a motor-car, and was under the impression that you take your seats, press the button, and the machine does the rest. Well, at last, on November 21, 1895, the thing arrived at Portsmouth Town station.

"I had been told in a letter from the maker that to start the engine you had to turn the flywheel towards you, which I did until darkness overtook me. The only result was a pair of worn-out gloves."

Mr. Koosens here seems to have found the trouble too much for him, for he says: "And now I think perhaps it would be better to quote my wife's diary (I don't keep one myself)."

"*November 23*—Took train to Lee and tried to make our motor work; wouldn't; came home at five.

"*November 24*—Awfully cold; played with our motor—no result.

"*November 25*—After luncheon saw to our motor, but didn't get it out of shed.

"*November 26*—Drove to Lee and took Smith and Penning (engineers); Penning spent the day on his back with no results.

"*November 27*—Drove to Lee; first we

9

drove to T. White & Co. to see about oil, but they gave us five gallons of the stuff costers burn in their flares over their barrows, which messed up our motor, which of course didn't go.

"*November 30* – Motor *went* with benzoline for first time; awfully pleased.

"*December 2* – Waiting for new oil from Bowley & Son.

"*December 9* – Drove to Lee at 10; motor sparked at once and went well. After lunch started for home in motor-car; came round by Fareham; had lovely drive; police spotted us; awful crowd followed us at Cosham; had to beat them off with umbrella.

"*December 10* – Policeman called at 1:30, took our names *re* driving through Fareham without red flag ahead.

"*December 13* – Went drive round common; tyre came off; sent her to Penning.

"*December 16* – Took train to Fareham; met Hobbs (Hide and Hobbs, solicitors) and Mr. Heckett, and proceeded to Court House; filthy place; Hobbs spoke up well for motors (see police reports). Silly old magistrate fined us one shilling and costs, 15s. 7d.

"*December 27* – Frightened an unattended horse attached to a milk-cart, which bolted and sent the milk-cans flying in all directions.

"*December 31* – Straps slipped badly, had to get them tightened.

"*January 4, 1896* – Lost nut off air valve; pushed home.

"*January 6* – Stuck again, small tube supplying petrol to carburetter choked.

"*January 14* – Motor got stuck; made noises; sent her to Penning's.

"*January 19* – Moted to Eastney Lock; Jack got out to hold unattended horses, and I drove the car into the curb and smashed frame. Shoved into a stable close by.

"*April 14* – Accumulators gave out,

bumped them into Penning's to get charged.

"*April 19* – Took fresh accumulators out to Lee, but they would not make the engine go, so took them back again.

"*April 22* – Took accumulators out again and started at once; did 30 miles for first time in 3½ hours."

And so on. . . .

If a man born in the mid-1800's couldn't adapt himself to the fast-moving machinery of the 1900's, his son born in, say, 1885, could. And quickly, too. By 1907 or so, when cars had become reasonably sophisticated and reliable, a new generation which had reached maturity along with the motorcar not only had some mechanical sense, but was also crazy about cars. If papa had enough money (decent cars were still for the well-to-do), Junior had himself a wonderful time on the road.

What was a fine car of those happy days like? I'm not talking about the myriad cheap "Everyman's" cars which speculators quickly assembled in hopes (often realized) of sudden riches, but about the well-engineered, staunchly put together, expensive machines of the period.

Such an automobile had a longish wheelbase – 120 inches or more – both to allow for a side entrance to its commodious tonneau and to prevent the pitching and directional instability from which earlier, short-wheelbase machines suffered. (A rear entrance had previously been *de rigueur* because a rear wheel, and ofttimes its driving chain, had blocked the area where a side door might have been placed.)

The chassis frame was in most cases a steel pressing and was sprung on semielliptic leaf springs, although full elliptics were not uncommon in the rear. (The wood chassis had just about disappeared, except in odd in-

10

Period literature shows how automobiles captured America's affections and became essential part of lives widened by new possibilities of travel.

stances like the American air-cooled Franklin, which retained it for some twenty-five years.) Wheels were normally wood-spoked. The wire wheel was still a rarity, although some of the earliest cars had used them.

Big, four-cylinder engines, rated at from 35 to 50 horsepower, were almost universal, although Napier and Rolls-Royce in England had started a trend toward sixes. Their cubic capacity was from 4 to 7 litres, a size which, oddly, is about the same as that in the full-sized Detroit car of today. By 1907 engines could be run at varying speeds controlled by their carburetor throttles. Inflexible engines running at an almost constant speed were a thing of the past. Now a hand control on a steering-wheel quadrant, or a foot accelerator, varied the speed of the car. It was no longer necessary to shift gears in order to speed up or slow down. The gearshift had become more a means of starting from rest or of getting more power to the wheels on hills.

The normal gearbox (as opposed to devices with a multiplicity of clutches and constant-mesh gears as in the Welch, an American car of quixotic design) had three speeds plus reverse, all slid into mesh by a satisfyingly hand-filling brass lever, whose manipulation still required a certain finesse.

By 1907, shaft drive from the gearbox to the driving wheels aft was quite usual, but the designers of many powerful machines still put their faith in drives with delightfully brutal-sounding chains transmitting power from the gearbox to great sprockets on the peripheries of the rear brake drums. Front-wheel brakes were in the not-too-distant future.

This, briefly and basically, was about what the mechanism of a typical $4,000 car was like sixty years ago.

How did such a car perform on the road?

Let's say it is a springtime Sunday in 1907, and you're about to set forth on your weekly motoring excursion. First you check to see that your car is supplied with gasoline. You remove a front seat cushion to expose the gas tank, whose filler cap you unscrew. You poke a clean stick into the opening, then withdraw it to see how much is wetted with fuel. To check the amount of oil in the crankcase you reach under the car, turn a valve. If oil drips out, all is well. You check the water in the radiator. After that you walk around the car giving the grease cups a turn or two. Now you're almost ready to start the engine. You open the hood and squirt a few drops of gasoline into the petcocks fitted to the cylinders. Now you set the spark control on the quadrant above the steering column at full retard and the throttle control about two-thirds open (this varied according to the vagaries of your car). You switch on the ignition (usually by trembler coil or magneto or both). This is the time to grasp the nettle, the crank. If your engine is *au point,* a quick jerk-up sets it singing— but too fast. You rush back toward the steering column and as you almost close the hand throttle you advance the spark a bit. The engine settles down, runs sweetly, and you and your passengers climb aboard. The open road lies ahead.

It's delightful. There's no traffic to speak of. The car swings along on its supple springs, comfortably, quietly. Minor bumps and hollows mean little to the big wheels.

You sit high and mighty on your diamond-pleated leather armchair. Your view in every direction is magnificent. Hedges and fences are beneath you, not next to you. You look over them into people's yards. The car's headlights, fenders, even the front wheels,

13

TOP: *A conclave of early machines prior to a 1900 British Trial. Among them are a Daimler, Benz, Peugeot, Panhard, another Benz.* BOTTOM: *Designer Laurence H. Pomeroy Sr. at the wheel of the first production Prince Henry Vauxhall at Lynmouth, England, in 1911.*

are perfectly visible. But to see rearwards you must turn your head. The rear-view mirror is still in the future.

You have to steer carefully, for just a slight turn of the small, thick, mahogany steering wheel makes for a big movement of your front wheels. Gear-shifting for hills is precise and easy, for the teeth on the gear wheels are big and wide-spaced. The gears, however, are by no means silent.

The gears aren't used much anyhow. You don't drop down into a lower gear to accelerate, but only when you slow down in traffic or when climbing a hill. And even this is unusual in a 50-horsepower car whose engine develops enough low-speed torque to make shifting almost unnecessary except when starting from rest. The clutch, which consists of two conical, leather-lined members sliding each into the other, is remarkably smooth, especially if you have remembered now and then to treat the leather with castor oil. If the clutch slips, you shake a little fuller's earth onto the leather for a better grip. Some cars—a minority—use other forms of clutches: expanding shoes inside a drum, very much on the order of an internally expanding brake, or multiple-disc clutches which do their work in a bath of oil. If you drive a Mercedes, the clutch consists of a coil spring encircling the drive shaft. When released by the foot pedal, it decreases its diameter to grip the shaft.

The brass controls on the quadrant growing out of the hub of the steering wheel are meant to be used. One controls the carburetor throttle and was used to adjust the speed of the car until the foot accelerator became fashionable. But you still use it to set the idling speed or, if you're on a long, flat, straight road, you use it instead of the foot accelerator. Once set for the speed you want, the notches on the quadrant will hold it in position.

The other control advances and retards the ignition. When you started, you retarded it. Once on the road at speed, you moved it almost to full advance and left it there. But climbing a hill the engine starts to slow, and you slowly move the lever toward "retard" again to match the engine speed.

The two-wheel brakes are good enough. The light traffic requires no panic stops. And brakes have improved these last few years. They hold going backwards, too, and cars no longer require a sprag (a stout iron rod hinged beneath the car) to dig into the ground in case you start rolling rearwards down a hill.

But you're still on a macadamized road and inevitably you'll be running on rough dirt roads this day, too. For paved highways are few in 1907. And dirt roads mean that you'll be trailed by a long plume of dust, some of which will be sucked forward into your car. (That's why automobilists envelop themselves in dusters.) Almost inevitably, too, you'll have tire trouble, for tires, like roads, have not kept up with the quick advances in comfort, handling, and reliability of cars.

In addition to the pleasurable excitements of actually driving his car, the autoist of 1907 had a host of delightful devices to amuse him during the pursuit of his hobby —for automobilism was still a hobby, not a necessity.

Consider the fun he had with lamps. Fancy headlights and sidelamps and taillights were a form of jewelry with which the autoist loved to bedizen his gas-engined mistress. If an autoist didn't think the headlights with which his car was delivered were spectacular

16

This early French poster for De Dion cars foreshadowed the questionable pleasures of family motoring. Note that gearshift lever is on the steering column. Vehicles in background are also De Dions: two tricycles, a quadricycle, and a bus.

enough to impress his friends, a dozen American manufacturers were eager to supply him with brass jewels in a hundred shapes. And if domestic headlights seemed too ordinary, American agents could quickly supply him with more flamboyant *projecteurs* direct from Paris, France.

Such headlights burned acetylene gas. Earlier types — self-generators — contained a compartment into which the motorist placed a quantity of calcium carbide. A neighboring compartment was filled with water. To manufacture the acetylene gas the autoist opened a valve which allowed water to drip into the carbide. Now he had gas. Next he opened the glass front of each headlamp and with a match lit the gas as it escaped from its Y-shaped burner. All this wasn't quite so easy as it sounds. Used carbide formed a stony mass in its container which continually had to be cleaned. Burners clogged and their pinhole openings required cleaning, too — with a specially devised wire "pricker," a supply of which was carried in the tool box. And if it were a windy night, matches as well as burners blew out before the headlight door could be closed.

The "self-generator" headlight soon gave way to a similar appliance in which the generator sat in a brass cylinder on the running board. Gas was sent to the headlights through thin copper pipes and rubber tubes. Later it was possible to buy compressed acetylene gas in "Prestolite" cylinders.

By our standards, acetylene headlights were ridiculously dim. But to quiet those who complained of being blinded by their brilliance, dimmers (small black discs) could be swung in front of the burners by means of a dashboard control to blank out the fearsome glare. It was also possible to light the burners by remote control. A device

inside the headlights made an electric spark which, it was hoped, would ignite the gas. But unless the button for this automated lighter was pressed at the crucial moment, the headlight, filled with gas, could destroy itself in a shattering explosion.

Your pre-Kaiser War motorist loved horns, too. Although the very early cars gave warning of their approach by means of bells, the rubber-bulbed horn (sometimes squeezed by the driver's foot) soon became the accepted form of noisemaker, especially since it allowed the autoist to embellish his vehicle with a yard of so of brass trumpet twisted round and round upon itself — the more twists, the more desirable the horn. Another conceit was the boa-constrictor horn, which was no more than a long horn fitted with an open-mouthed brazen serpent's head lying supine upon a fender. Still other means of destroying the quiet of the countryside were the various types of exhaust horn. These, which sometimes looked like bundles of organ pipes, were connected with the exhaust pipe beneath the car. Merely by pulling a control, the driver could make them bray most melodiously.

There were other fripperies for the autoist of the Teddy Roosevelt era. One, which I have always fancied, but have been able to find only in pictures, was a communication system between the nabob in the rear of a closed town car and the chauffeur up front. Speaking tubes and even electric telephones didn't compare to it for letting the paid driver know that he was of a class with whom one did not converse. The occupant in the rear had a keyboard with buttons marked: Go! Stop! Turn right! Turn left! Slow down! Faster! Go home! The driver, of course, had a duplicate board upon which these commands registered. Neat?

Brakes on this 1908 rear-entrance Peerless negotiating the steep incline to the ferryboat must have been better than those of some other vehicles which had earlier attempted the hill. Note their erratic wheel tracks.

Almost until the 1914 war, cars generally were not too unlike our imaginary tourer of 1907, at least in their chassis design. Body styles did, however, change considerably. Front doors appeared and it became stylish for the sides of the body to have a straight line from cowl to derriere.

In 1912, electric starting and lighting revolutionized the world of the automobile. Women could now use gasoline cars without having to crank their engines. This not only doomed the ladies' electric autos, but put an end to the motorcar's role as a pure article of pleasure. Although future millions upon millions of automobiles would be little more than household appliances, a tiny fraction of this multitude of machines would be built for those special people who delighted in the contemplation of beautifully built mechanism and imaginatively designed bodywork, and who knew how good a car ought to feel in action on the open highway.

INVI

GB

TF 5198

INVICTA

The low-chassis, S-type Invicta was like a woman you could love and hate at the same time. You could love its looks, its low, low build, its unique and beautifully shaped radiator sitting well back between its front wheels, its long multi-louvered hood lined with rivets accenting its crisp hard-edged shape. You could, most of the time, be happy with the way an Invicta went, too. It had (for its day) fine acceleration (0 to 60 in about 14 seconds), high speed (in the 90's), and it generally went where you pointed it. And it emitted a fine down-in-the-throat roar from its outside exhaust pipes, à la Mercedes-Benz.

You could hate the Invicta, however, for one miserable vice. For no reason at all and without warning, its after-quarters would sometimes want to be in front, and you could spin in a most horrifying manner.

This S-type, 100-mph (an exaggeration, I fear) Invicta was the last of the line, except for one of the same name which died young in the forties; Buicks don't count. Earlier Invictas hadn't much character and the Invicta name, if not for the S-type, would merely be another in the list of half-forgotten marques.

The precursors of the low-chassis sports Invicta first took the road in 1925. In those days they were quiet, moderately well-built touring machines with no aspirations toward sporting use. They were at that time too high, too heavy, and had 3-litre Meadows engines in conventional, ladder-type chassis frames.

But Captain Noël Macklin (later Lord Macklin), who was the power behind Invictas, was determined to make them famous. To this end he had an energetic lady, Miss Violet Corderey, drive an Invicta around the world and also engage in some record breaking. She took the 25,000-kilometer record at 55.7 mph and won the Dewar Trophy for running 5,000 miles at 70.7 mph at the Montlhéry track near Paris.

In 1928, a larger engine of 4½ litres was installed in what was essentially the same light and whippy chassis. Road holding was less than perfect and the 1929 model was given a stronger, stiffer chassis and a deeper, lower radiator. Known as the Invicta Sports and capable of about 80 mph, this "high chassis" Invicta was still a touring car, not a sports machine.

It wasn't until September of 1930 that the low-chassis, 100-mph, S-type Invicta arrived on the scene. Now, at last, Invicta had done it. Now it was a motorcar to make sporting drivers itch with acquisitiveness.

The new Invicta was lower than almost any car built. Too low, perhaps. It had a chassis frame of prodigious strength. Its springs, flat and stiff, were underslung aft. Steering was by Marles. André Telecontrol shock absorbers were fitted at each corner.

The 4½-litre, six-cylinder Meadows engine was beefed up with stronger rods, although it still had only four main bearings. Ignition was by coil and Rotax magneto. It breathed through twin S.U. carburetors and pushed out about 135 bhp. It was still, however, not unlike the engine Meadows built for trucks and, later on, for British military vehicles. The idea of using a tough truck engine in a sports car wasn't unique with the Invicta people. Delahaye, for instance, also used a truck engine, but it must be admitted that the Delahaye power plant, with its seven main bearings, was a much smoother affair. When you approached 4000 rpm on an Invicta, the engine began to feel a mite unhappy.

This bald recital of the Invicta's specification makes it sound almost prosaic, which it certainly was not. It had more lovely little

22

PRECEDING PAGES: 1932 4½-litre S-type low-chassis Invicta. Donald Healey drove a similar machine to first place in 1931 Monte Carlo Rally. Called 100-MPH Invicta, it was capable of slightly over 90 mph. Beautifully built low-chassis type did not survive 1935.

*Low-set radiator, big wheels, and low, 4½-inch
ground clearance gave the Invicta a look of stability
it unfortunately did not have. But
chassis frame had tremendous strength, brakes and steering
were precise. Headlights on this car are incorrect.*

features than almost any car I've known. To wit: The beautifully shaped radiator shell, with its built-in stone guard, was mounted on a pair of black rubber handballs, which were neatly embedded in hemispherical castings attached to the radiator and the chassis. A dual fuel-feed system was employed, using either an electric pump or air pressure in the giant rear tank, which boasted a huge airtight filler cap. If you wanted to use the electric pump, you pulled a switch. To use air pressure you pumped up two pounds (shown on a dashboard gauge) by means of a hand pump under the dash. Each system used a separate set of exquisitely fitted and plated fuel pipes, which you chose by operating a delightful system of dash-controlled valves.

The instrument panel was attached to a big aluminum casting—the firewall—by means of two aluminum brackets. Invisible, unless you either removed the body or lay flat on the floor to look up at them, they were laboriously cut out to spell the name "Invicta." On the instrument panel there was also a plug-in fuse which could be removed to cut out the generator, making it possible to run the car without its battery, hand-cranking to start.

Even the gear-changing system looked unusual. An aluminum tunnel above the floor carpet carried the shifting rods to the hefty right-hand gear lever in its plated gate. Another nice touch was its starter switch. To start you pulled up the horn button.

I first saw my Invicta—No. S 155—on May 10, 1940, the terrible day Hitler attacked in the West. A young Englishman had driven it from Canada to Zumbach's, that wonderful foreign-car service emporium of prewar days, for servicing. I was enchanted, but I didn't imagine that three years later, after both the Englishman and I were in the army, I'd be able to buy it for $400. I kept it for seven happy years and still regret trading it in on a Riley—of all things!

Although the Invicta had its little quirks, it was a delight on the road. Fast—I could almost always out-accelerate and outmaneuver elephantine 540K Mercedes-Benz's and 4¼-litre Rolls-Bentleys. (But 2.3 blown Alfas were another story!) Steering and brakes—if heavy—were always precise. Gear-changing was a pleasure. But besides its tendency to swap ends, the Invicta had another foible which terrified me until I learned to cope with it. At 50 mph or so, a horrifying, eyeball-rattling wheel wobble would set in. Tightening the telecontrol shock absorbers effected an instant cure. The Invicta's extreme lowness (4½-inch ground clearance) was sometimes a nuisance, too, especially when a hump in a driveway wiped off the grease nipples on the brake cross shaft.

Invictas did well in competition, however. In 1931 Donald Healey set off single-handed in the Monte Carlo Rally. Almost at his starting point in northern Sweden, Healey skidded and hit a pole hard enough to turn his rear axle askew. This set the rear brakes solid. Healey disconnected them, drove across Europe, across the Alps in midwinter, to win the rally outright. Raymond Mays for some years held the hill-climb record at Shelsley-Walsh in his specially prepared Invicta. A. C. Lace, in 1933, attained a higher lap speed over the Ards circuit in Ireland than Sir Henry Birkin in his famed 4½-litre Bentley.

But by 1935, the low-chassis Invicta was dead. Other types which had been built, among them a blown 1½-litre Blackburne-engined car, failed also. A super-Invicta

with a big twin-cam engine, which was still going through its birth pangs when production ended, never appeared.

What killed the Invicta? Two things: exaggerated gossip about its tail-wagging and, of course, the world depression which dried up sales and money for further development.

In 1947 a new company tried to revive the Invicta. Their car, yclept the Black Prince, had a beautifully built 3-litre, twin-cam engine, a sliding-pillar, independent front suspension, and lovely coachwork. But it was saddled with a wondrously complex autotransmission, the Brockhouse Hydrokinetic Turbo Torque Converter, and an astronomical price tag. Not many were sold.

TOP: *A 4½-litre Invicta in a British hill climb event at Prescott.*
LEFT: *Invicta cockpit. Right-hand gear lever connects with gearbox via transverse tunnel. Horn button also activates starter.*
RIGHT: *Six-cylinder Meadows engine had pushrod-overhead valves, twin S.U. carburetors, four main bearings. S.U. fuel pumps are a modification.*

Talbot-Lago

PRECEDING PAGES: *1939 Type 150C-SS Talbot-Lago with Partout coupé body. This model had semi-automatic Wilson gearbox, 4-litre engine, and top speed near 115 mph. Chassis was independently suspended in front by transverse spring.*

ABOVE: *Details from Talbot-Lago Type 150-SS Figoni and Falaschi-bodied convertible on page 31. These Type 150's still had single valve rocker boxes instead of twin boxes on postwar models. Note triple Solex carburetors.*

Talbot-Lago It must have been about 1937 at the auto show in Grand Central Palace that I first saw a Talbot-Lago. Exiled upstairs among the spark intensifiers and magic cleaning preparations, it stood not far from the used but immaculate Type 51 Bugatti then owned by Maclure Halley. Nearby, too, the not-yet-famous Buckminster Fuller showed plaster models of his ill-fated Dymaxion Transport.

That early Talbot-Lago, although it had as voluptuously curvilinear a body by Figoni and Falaschi as any car-bemused schoolboy might try to sketch, somehow didn't excite us as much as it should have. For apart from its curly shape it seemed, under its skin, a mite crude compared to the Breguet-watch precision of the Bugatti's mechanism.

This Talbot-Lago was Antony Lago's first essay in building a car bearing, at least in part, his own name. Lago, an Italian, had been working with cars for a long time. He had held an important engineering post with the builders of the Wilson pre-selector gearbox, a semiautomatic transmission he would remain faithful to for years to come. Later he joined the English division of the corporately complex STD combine. I'll not try to sort this out; hardly anybody can. STD stood for Sunbeam-Talbot-Darracq, an Anglo-French mishmash of companies which sold Sunbeams and Talbots in England and Darracqs and Talbots in France (the Talbots in England were called Tall-butts, in France Tahl-bows). Neither the English nor the French sections of the company were doing too well, the French branch being the sicker member. Lago was therefore ordered to Suresnes to try to effect a cure.

While Lago was at Suresnes, the Rootes group bought out the English part of the company and Lago assumed control of the Talbot-Darracq complex in France.

Tony Lago was an enthusiast. He loved luxurious high-performance cars. The rather dull machines Talbot-Darracq was building were hardly his pieces of cake. Starting with the Talbot-Darracq Type K78, which had a six-cylinder pushrod ohv engine, he set to work. He had his engineer, Walter Becchia, design an ingenious new hemispherical combustion-chambered head, whose valves were worked by crosswise pushrods. Twin carburetors, usually Solexes, were fitted and in this form the 4-litre engine pushed out almost 140 hp at 4000 rpm.

The chassis of this Type 150-SS was typically French in its toughness and was independently sprung in front by means of a transverse spring. And Wilson gearboxes were, of course, standard. Most of these cars had haute-couture Figoni coachwork.

But Tony Lago wasn't satisfied with merely fast and beautiful sports-touring cars. He wanted to go racing, and wooed the French crack, René Dreyfus, away from the Scuderia Ferrari to manage his new racing team. In their first race, the French Grand Prix in 1936, three Talbot-Lagos came in eighth, ninth, and tenth. The next year in the French G.P. they placed first, second, third, and fifth. In the British Tourist Trophy at Donington Park, Gianfranco Comotti and René Lebegue made it first and second. But Lago really didn't have a chance to go on winning, for those were the grim prewar days when the Germans in their swastikaed Auto-Unions and Mercedes-Benz's almost always came in first.

As an Italian, Lago was safe for a time after France fell, but racing had stopped in Europe. Lago then sent two of his racing Talbots, bored out to 4½ litres, to America for the 1941 Indianapolis "500." Unfortunately, Lebegue and Trevoux couldn't qualify them and the cars, after running in the Pike's Peak hill climb and doing no better than third and fourth, just sat around gathering dust. They were then sold at auction, and for the ridiculous price of $400 Robert Grier of New York got one of them. The other later became the property of the noted Zora Arkus-Duntov, who is now chief engineer of Corvette Sting-Ray development. Both of these machines still had the cross-pushrod heads and turned out about 250 bhp at a redline of 4900. Arkus-Duntov modified his by fitting a crankshaft damper of his own design which enabled him to rev at 5200 without breaking up the crankshaft. Oddly, it was the bottom end of the Talbot that was delicate, not its valve gear.

It was the postwar Talbot-Lagos that made the name great. These now had twin camshafts (not overhead), which worked the valves, still by pushrods, from twin rocker boxes which looked like the housings for overhead camshafts. In racing trim these engines developed close to 300 bhp.

Lago was almost unique among car constructors. He was of the opinion that when cars gained fame through racing, it was only right that the selfsame engine—detuned—be installed in the cars that could be bought off the showroom floor. Few manufacturers are ever this honest. Mercedes-Benz, for example, although it has gained kudos from racing, wouldn't dream of installing a Grand Prix engine in one of its passenger cars. Its G.P. engines seldom have the least resemblance to anything you can buy. They couldn't possibly operate in a car meant for street use, anyhow.

But in the late forties the 4½-litre Talbot-Lago engine was used for G.P. racing. In the hands of Louis Rosier and his son, it won

five G.P. races against blown Alfas, Maseratis, and Ferraris; since it used far less fuel, it could keep running while the thirsty super-charged machines were in the pits.

The same engine was used in sports-car racing. A 4½-litre-engined car won at Le Mans in 1950, when Rosier *et fils* broke every record for the course. And Talbot missed winning only by a whisker again in 1952.

There's a sad tale in connection with that Le Mans of 1952. Pierre Levegh entered a Talbot-Lago and insisted he would drive the twenty-four hours without relief. At the end of twenty-three hours he was in the lead, twenty-odd miles ahead of the Mercedes in second place. But he was by then an exhausted automaton. Stopping in the pits for fuel he acted dazed. He did not even recognize his own pit crew. His wife and Lago begged him to allow a relief driver to take over but Levegh brushed them aside and took off. Forty-four minutes from the end of the race, Levegh muffed a gear change—easy to do with a Wilson box if you can't remember which gear you're in—over-revved, and blew the engine.

The same 4½-litre engine was used in the Grand Sport road car, but developed 190 bhp—and they were full-grown horses, because with moderately heavy and lush bodywork such a "street" Talbot-Lago was capable of 125 mph—very good for 1950.

I almost succeeded in buying such a Grand Sport Lago in 1951. I had come upon it in a garage next door to Zumbach's, in whose charge it was. Immediately in love with it and discovering that it was for sale, I heckled Werner Maeder (then Zumbach's foreman and now its head) into letting me try it. It was then and still is one of the very greatest cars I've ever driven. It had coupé bodywork of unsurpassable luxury. Even its

30

headlining was of pigskin. With its short chassis and quick steering it handled like a racing machine. And it could *go!* But unlike so many super-sports machines its engine just loafed along. Its high-geared rear axle gave it 27 mph at 1000 rpm. At 80 (the highest speed we dared on New York's West Side highway), the rev counter read under 3000. Zero to 60 took about 9 seconds. And despite the dubious looks you get when you talk of Wilson pre-selector gearboxes, the one on the Lago was lovely. Traveling along in high gear it was merely necessary to think ahead and decide what lower gear I wanted to use next. I then placed the small lever on the steering-column quadrant in that gear, say third. Coming into a corner I merely stamped on a pedal (similar to a clutch pedal) and I was in that gear fast, *now!*

But to my continuing regret I never did get that car. We couldn't immediately find its owner. In a nervous snit, wanting to do *something*, I phoned the Hollywood dealer who had originally sold it, ostensibly to get

more information about it but mostly, really, because like a frustrated lover I just had to talk to someone about it. The dealer told me I'd be getting a wonderful buy for the $5,500 I had offered. Then he turned around, found the owner, and took the car away for $6,500. I'm still desolated.

Tony Lago made other models, too: the Record, a bit less potent; the Baby, with a 120 hp, four-cylinder engine; and, toward the end, a BMW V-8 engined car called the Lago America.

But the Talbot-Lago is no more. Like Delahaye and Delage and Hotchkiss, Talbot-Lago could not withstand the antic French income-tax system which considers a man conspicuously wealthy and subject to increased taxation if he owns a high-priced car. Nor, unhappily, was Antony Lago ever able to sell many of his expensive products in the United States.

In 1959 Simca absorbed Automobiles Talbot-Darracq S.A. And in 1960 Tony Lago died, too.

LANCHESTER

LANCHESTER No cars ever built were as brilliantly original as the early Lanchesters, nor was there ever a motorcar engineer as brilliantly original as their designer, Frederick Lanchester.

Lanchester, born in 1868, had the da Vinci kind of mind that is excited by many things. As early as the 1890's he delved into the mysteries of heavier-than-air flight. He interested himself in optics and photography, in music and poetry. And when he set his mind to designing a motorcar he did it in his own unique way, owing nothing to what others had done before.

There really hadn't been much done before, because Lanchester was already designing a car as early as 1894. But in a day when other designers were concerned with making improvements (and they were considerable, particularly in the case of the French Panhard-Levassor) on Daimler's motorized horse-carriages or Benz's belt-driven tricycles and quadricycles, Lanchester struck out along a unique course of his own.

In company with his brother George, Fred Lanchester built two experimental machines which incorporated his advanced ideas on what a motorcar should be. In 1899 the second of these won a special gold medal for running 68 miles at an average speed of 26 mph in the Richmond trial. It wasn't until 1901, however, that an actual production Lanchester took to the Queen's highway, for Fred Lanchester was a perfectionist who didn't start building cars for sale until an entire system of production had been worked out. He was the first to insist on fully interchangeable parts, before Henry Leland of Cadillac, who is usually credited with this, and long before Henry Ford. To this end it was necessary to design and build specialized machine tools, go and no-go gauges, special jigs, and all the devices which other manufacturers did not deem necessary until, years later, they turned to mass production.

How did Lanchester's 1901 car differ from others of its time? First, in a day when most car engines tried to shake themselves (and the cars they powered) to pieces, when lamps and fenders and passengers jiggled in a blur of vibration, Lanchester's opposed twin-cylinder engine (5¼-inch bore by 5 11/16 stroke) ran smoothly. The shaking caused by the unbalanced masses and the explosions of a two-cylinder engine was canceled out by using two crankshafts, one above the other, rotating in opposite directions. Each piston was connected to both crankshafts by means of three connecting rods, two of which connected with one crankshaft while the third rod connected with the other. The balanced crankshafts were geared together.

Ignition was by "make-and-break," but instead of the usual low-tension magneto, Lanchester designed a flywheel magneto not too unlike that used much later in the Model T Ford. (There's evidence that Henry Ford once took a hard look at Lanchester's magneto.) Low-tension ignition produces its spark, not by means of a spark plug, but by means of an igniter or switch inside the cylinder. When this switch is suddenly opened, usually by means of a cam-operated rod outside the cylinder, a spark jumps across the switch points. This worked fine on low-speed engines, but when the contacts burned or became dirty, it was necessary to dig out a wrench and unbolt the red-hot mechanisms for adjustment. Lanchester designed igniters which could be instantly removed and replaced by turning a cool mica handle. They were held in place like the breech blocks of field guns. Further, they had an external adjustment, so that the spark gaps could be

PRECEDING PAGES: 1913 Lanchester 38-hp six-cylinder
*Torpedo Tourer. On a fast corner one of these softly sprung
machines leans as if it were a small boat in a heavy
sea, yet car's occupants feel perfectly secure. One car like
this with slight modifications could exceed 90 mph.*

*Other views of 1913 Lanchester. Picture at
lower right shows how engine protrudes into driving
compartment between passengers and driver.
Many of these 38-hp chassis were fitted out as armored
cars for the British forces in World War I.*

BELOW: *1897 experimental Lanchester now in Science Museum in London.* RIGHT: *1900 Lanchester. This pre-production model already had Lanchester's side-lever steering which lay along the driver's forearm and gave much better control than ordinary tiller steering.*

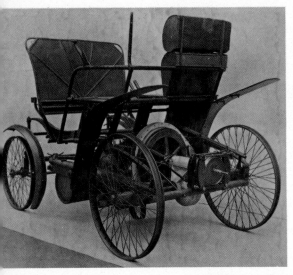

ABOVE: *Lanchester's twin cylinders each had two connecting rods which operated two crankshafts, thus engine was practically vibrationless.* RIGHT: *10-hp Lanchester which made nonstop run in 1903 London-Glasgow Trial. Frederick Lanchester is man in bowler hat.*

LEFT: *Early Lanchester tonneaus were entered from the rear. Top swung forward to let passengers in, not to prevent them from seeing where they were going.* BELOW: *Gear-changing and fuel-feed controls were between front seats. Steering lever is at full left lock.*

changed while the engine was running.

The first Lanchester production cars had air-cooled engines which put out about 10 bhp at 750 rpm—more at their peak of 1200 rpm. But various pundits sneered at air-cooling, so Lanchester, to satisfy those customers who listened to the experts, brought out a water-cooled version which developed two more horsepower—the power which the cooling fans had absorbed.

Turning up his nose at the curious and fussy devices which carbureted most engines of the time, Lanchester went back to an earlier, simpler system: the surface, or wick, carburetor. Instead of spraying globules of fuel which were mixed with air to form a more or less combustible mixture, the wick carburetor evaporated the gases from the fuel. Air was passed over these vapors and

40

the engine then sucked in the combustible fumes.

Don't imagine that the "wick" of a Lanchester carburetor looked like something stolen out of a kerosene lamp. It looked more like the business end of a floor mop, cut off from its handle and then stuck vertically in a brass pail. The pail was partly buried in the car's gas tank so there was no cloggable piping between the tank and the carburetor. They were all of a piece. The gas tank, a cylinder the full width of the rigid Lanchester chassis, formed one of its strong transverse members. But a Lanchester chassis was no ladderlike frame of pressed steel. It made up the lower half of the body, and the rigid aluminum and steel girders which formed its sides were no less than eighteen inches deep. The steel bed plate of the en-

RIGHT: *1912 38-hp six-cylinder Lanchester.*
Allowing engine to come back into driving compartment gave
rear passengers a luxurious amount of space.
Pre-World War I Lanchesters were thought unstylish by
those to whom short hoods denoted lack of power.

gine which lay amidships between the girders added additional stiffness.

Like many machines of its time the Lanchester had a planetary transmission, but it differed in quality and performance from the usual types as a marine chronometer differs from a three-dollar alarm clock. This transmission, plus an ingeniously combined clutch and brake, was joined to the underside of the engine and geared to the lower of the two engine crankshafts. Unlike most planetary systems, which usually had but two speeds, the Lanchester's had three speeds and these could be pre-selected in a similar manner to the much later Wilson gearbox.

Gear-shifting was easy, but the controls looked most unconventional. Between the driver's and front passenger's seat, on what Detroit would now call a "console," stood two short levers on quadrants and a small pre-selector, or "gear change trigger." Flicking these levers back and forth in various combinations, changed pre-selected gears , and applied powerful brakes if either big lever was pulled all the way back. The system was quiet; there was nothing to do with your feet except to depress the accelerator or the bulb horn. Later, to satisfy fearful customers Lanchester supplied optional foot brakes—discs, of all things! The first ever.

The rear wheels of the Lanchester were driven by a particularly quiet and efficient worm drive and, remarkably, the wheels ran on splined shafts and roller bearings, the very first use of such now commonplace components. Lanchester had, in fact, to make his own roller bearings and design his own machinery to cut splines.

Lanchesters had unusually soft springs. They were never designed for sporting use (a 1901-1905 Lanchester would, however, reach 40 mph), and the spring rates were based on the rise and fall of a man walking. Further, the seats were positioned so that their occupants' eye level would be at the same height as the average person afoot. Lanchester believed that this would be more natural and make it easier to judge distances.

Until long after other makers had abandoned tillers, Lanchester persisted in the use of such wheel-less steering. But his system was entirely different from the usual stalk grow-

ing out of the floor. His tiller, or "side lever," as he called it, lay alongside the right arm of the driver's seat. It was very quick and direct and it felt natural. As the Lanchester instruction book said: "Experience has shown that it is one of the best forms of steering for encountering unexpected obstacles for the same reason that the bath-chair tiller proved to be one of the worst and a car fitted with our side-lever steering tends always to steer in smooth curves, and to oversteer is almost a physical impossibility owing to the centrifugal force acting on the driver's body tending always to moderate his steering effort."

The bodywork of an early Lanchester was also unconventional. If it was necessary to work on the machinery, all of it could be removed in pieces in minutes, and without tools. Going back, each part locked the preceding part in place. Even the method of entering to the front seats was a delight. You swung the patent-leather dashboard forward. This then lifted the front fenders out of the way and you stepped in. The tonneau, as was usual before 1905, had a rear door.

Of all the cars of those early days, I do believe it's these Lanchesters that fascinate me most and make me most covetous.

In 1905 Lanchesters became more conventional, but only slightly. In that year a new 20-hp model with a vertical four-cylinder engine appeared. But Lanchester wasn't about to put his passengers behind a big hood. He built his engine narrow and set it between the front seats. Thus he saved several feet of length and was able to furnish a really commodious rear compartment with extra-wide side doors. In 1906 a 28-hp six-cylinder engine became available. But the side-mounted tiller, the wick carburetor, the planetary gears (now controlled by a more

normal single lever) still remained. In 1907, if you insisted, you could have wheel steering. In 1909 the side-lever steering finally disappeared; the cars by then were getting too heavy for tiller control.

At the time of World War I, the company directors, a shortsighted and penny-pinching crew, succeeded in pressuring George Lanchester, who for some years had been running the works, into abandoning the engine-between-the-seats Lanchester.

They, and many misguided customers, thought that a car with a long hood out front would be less "odd looking." So the Lanchester from that time on looked like any other big, expensive car. The wick carburetor went, but the transmission and worm-gear rear axle remained.

During the war Lanchester was the only British company besides Rolls-Royce to successfully build armored cars. They upheld their reputations beautifully on the long, cold Russian front, but, alas, unlike Rolls-Royce, they had no Lawrence of Arabia to sing their praises. He might have, had not the ship bearing the Lanchesters to the Middle East been torpedoed by the Germans.

After the war Lanchester continued to build fine motorcars; one, the six-cylinder 40 hp with inclined valves and an overhead camshaft, was capable of some 80 mph. Later, in 1928, a straight-eight—one of the finest cars of all time—was produced. But these and the other lovely machines built in the twenties and thirties lacked the character and individuality of Lanchester's earlier productions.

In 1931 Lanchester, like Bentley, was foundering. Daimler took over the company and continued to build cars called "Lanchesters." But they weren't really Lanchesters any more.

In 1914 *George Lanchester gave in to the dictates of fashion (and his board of directors) and produced a conventional-looking car.*
TOP: *The prototype* 1914 *Sporting Forty.* CENTER:
A coupe of the twenties. The round porthole in the radiator shows water level.
BOTTOM: *Miss Nancy Lanchester in a 1930 30-hp sports model.*

Hispano-Suiza

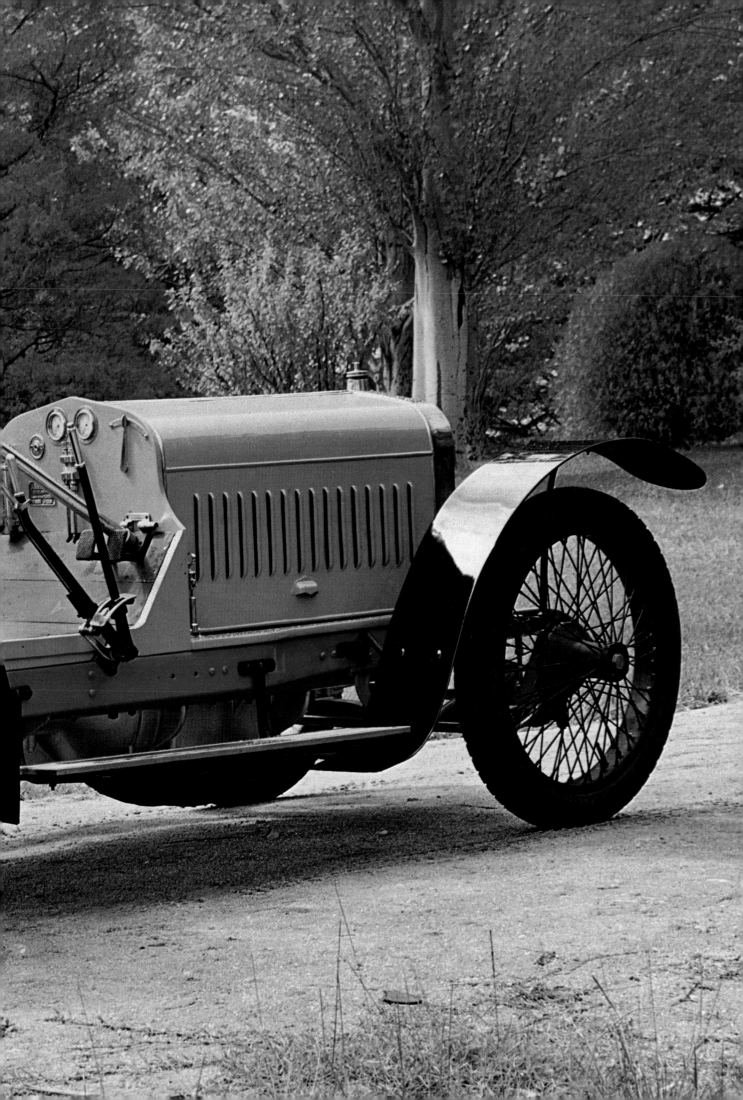

PRECEDING PAGES: *His Most Catholic Majesty Alfonso XIII, last Bourbon king of Spain, was so pleased by racing victories of four-cylinder T-15 Hispano-Suiza that he allowed it to be named for him. This 1912 Alfonso has non-standard fenders.*

ABOVE: *Paul Zucarelli driving the prototype of the later Alfonso Hispano-Suiza in 1910 Coupe des Voiturettes at Boulogne. For first time a four-cylinder car outran long-stroke one- and two-cylinder machines which had dominated that race.*

Hispano-Suiza

If you're that rare man who has a superabundance of pounds or dollars or lire, and if, furthermore, you're the sporting type, you can buy yourself a Ferrari. If you're of a more stately turn of mind, you might choose a closed Silver Shadow Rolls-Royce. Or you might even buy both, to use as your mood changes.

But there was a time in the golden twenties when one make of car, the Hispano-Suiza, suited the *grande dame* for an excursion to the *haut couturiers* of the Rue St. Honoré or the hectic young blade for a swift foray down the *routes nationales* toward a rendezvous in Biarritz. And the young man might use the selfsame machine, stripped of fenders and lamps, for a gruelling try at the Targa Florio as the aperitif king, André Dubonnet, did upon occasion.

This H6 37.2 Hispano-Suiza came upon the scene in that brightly optimistic time just after World War I. And, with its servo-operated four-wheel brakes, overhead-camshaft engine, and aluminum cylinder block, it was so far in advance of any other car as to shake even Rolls-Royce out of its patrician complacency. By comparison, the Rolls-Royce Silver Ghost was almost a relic—albeit a most desirable relic—of the Edwardian era. And the Hispano was built quite as precisely and as beautifully as the Royce.

The Hispano's wonderful engine was its great pride. As the instruction book says: "Its design is evolved from our aircraft engine, and it embodies its most distinctive and best features, based on the experience gained by us in the course of manufacturing nearly fifty thousand models in a period of four years, and of intensive service on all fronts...."

That aero engine had, indeed, been the Allies' most useful power plant. Superior to the German's Mercedes, it was simpler, too, with five hundred fewer parts. Further, it was only two-thirds as heavy as the German engine. It was built not only in Hispano's French factories, but also in the old Crane-Simplex factory in New Jersey and by Wright-Martin in Long Island City.

Flying their Hispano-engined Nieuports and Spads the aces of the western front—René Fonck, Guerin, Nungesser, Rickenbacker, Lufbery, and Guynemer—made their marks with famous victories over the German pilots. And it was Capitaine Georges Guynemer's squadron's device, the stork painted on the side of the Spads, which later became the Hispano's silvered radiator ornament—a dangerous one which threatened to impale careless pedestrians.

The aero engine had been a V-8, but the car engine was a monoblock six with a 100-mm bore and a 140-mm stroke. To quote the instruction book again: "The cylinders are a steel forging, threaded outwardly and screwed in an aluminum chamber or cooling jacket which is made corrosion-proof by a special process of enamelling under pressure...."

As in the aircraft engine, the valves were operated by an overhead camshaft driven by a vertical shaft. The cams pressed directly against the tops of the valves, which were fitted with hardened steel discs screwed to their stems. A special key was supplied to screw the discs in and out in a fashion similar to that which Alfa Romeo later used. Hispano-Suiza always insisted that their engines were extremely quiet. But, in fact, there was a discreet amount of clatter from the valve gear. After all, the clearance called for was a nice wide eighty-thousandths of an inch.

47

The engine was a showpiece in glossy black and aluminum but, unfortunately, its loveliest jewel, its seven-bearing crankshaft, was, perforce, hidden. This was carved out of a 700-pound steel billet and weighed but 90 pounds finished and polished.

Its compression ratio was low, a mere 4½ to 1, but, in spite of this, the 37.2 (R.A.C. rating) put out 135 horsepower at 2400 rpm and no less than 120 horsepower at 2000 rpm. This was enough to propel a light-bodied chassis (which only weighed 2500 pounds) at more than 90 mph. The larger-engined 8-litre Boulogne model (known as the 45 hp) would easily better 100 mph.

Hispanos had some intriguing features. Two batteries were fitted and the exquisite switch panel on the instrument board allowed you to use either one—or both for starting in winter when their strength was down. The fuse box, behind a glass panel, showed a tiny light for each fuse. If a fuse was burned out, its light went out, too.

The Hispano's four-wheel brakes were far better than anyone dreamed possible forty-five years ago (they'd even be quite good today). They not only had iron liners inside light-alloy finned drums, but their application was aided by a servo-mechanism driven from the side of the gearbox. Rolls-Royce later used a similar rig under license from Hispano.

It must have been sheer heaven to drive an open, light-bodied Hispano on those long, straight, tree-lined *routes nationales* of forty years ago. For, many years later, a much-used 37.2 which I had the good fortune to drive in the crowded environs of New York proved to me that there has seldom existed a big car with such delightful road manners. It steered quickly and to the inch—abetted no doubt by its thin (5½-inch) high-pressure (65-pound) tires. (Later models had fatter tires.) Its gearbox was fast and precise, but the Hispano's tremendous torque made its use almost redundant. Even with its high 3.37-to-1 rear axle, it was possible to slow in high gear to 4 mph and pick up cleanly and without fuss.

Again, I quote the instruction book: "The most perfect way of starting up on the level is to drive off on the second speed, practically without any gas admission. As soon as you feel that your car 'is moving,' shift the lever to the direct drive position and make no further change of gear, except in an emergency."

The big Hispano, especially in short-chassis Boulogne form, although never intended for racing, was often entered in competition by enthusiastic owners. André Dubonnet even entered his in the horrendous Targa Florio in 1924. Although entirely unsuited, it came in a creditable seventh. Dubonnet also once drove, complete with three passengers and their luggage, from Paris to Nice, 580 miles, in 12 hours and 35 minutes. Woolf Barnato, the famous "Bentley Boy," *averaged* 92.2 mph for 300 miles at Brooklands. And then there was that antic contest at Indianapolis in 1928, when C. F. Kettering, of General Motors, boasted that a Cadillac could beat a Rolls-Royce from Detroit to Dayton. It finally ended up as a twenty-four-hour match race for $25,000 between a Stutz Black Hawk and a Hispano. Unfortunately, it was no contest. The Stutz broke down early. The Hispano averaged over 70 for the twenty-four hours.

How did a French car get the name Hispano-Suiza—Spanish-Swiss? The answer is simple. The designer of the car was a Swiss, Mark Birkigt. The original company in 1904 was in Barcelona and called La Fabrica de

The H6 37.2 Hispano-Suiza was a car of dual
personality. It was, in the twenties, not only a near-perfect open sporting
machine, but was also well-suited as a coupé de ville
for formal town use. Above it appears as a double-cowl phaeton, a stuffy town
conveyance, and as a convertible (with decorative passenger).

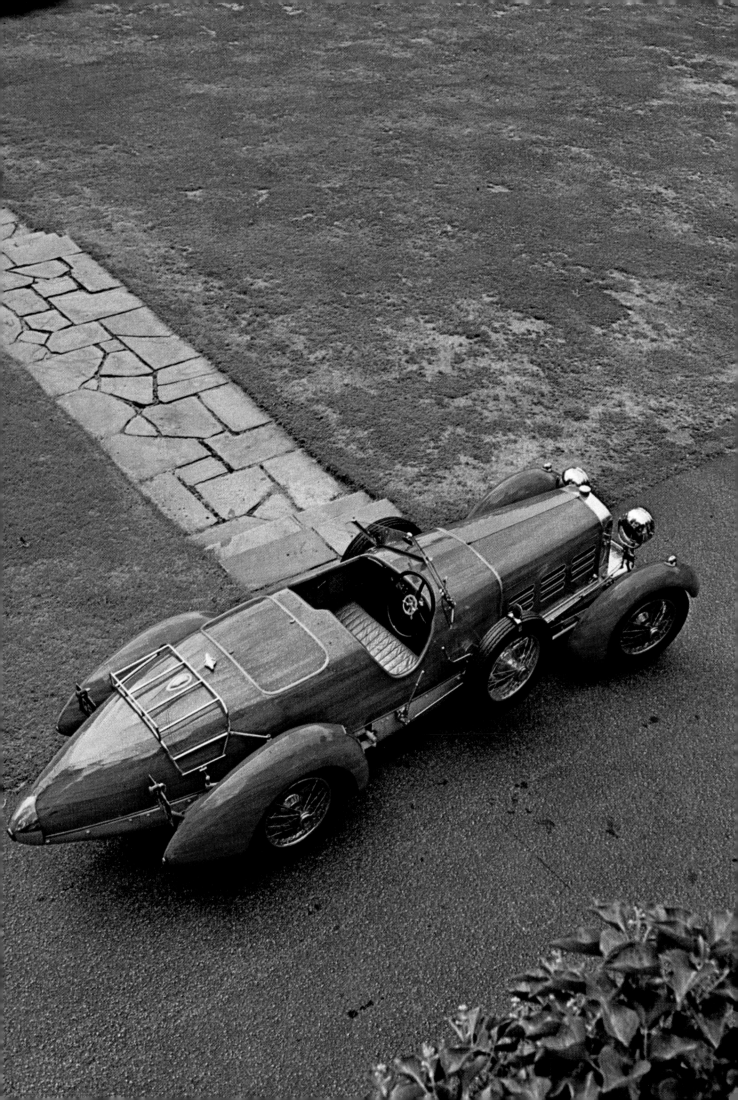

FAR LEFT: *A more powerful model of 37.2-hp Hispano-Suiza was the Boulogne, with an R.A.C. rating of 45 hp on a shorter chassis. This Boulogne has a speedboat-like body built of tulipwood strips fastened with thousands of copper rivets. Wooden teardrop fenders replace original metal ones.* LEFT: *Other aspects of Boulogne Hispano.*

LEFT: *Giant twelve-cylinder 11-litre Type 68 Hispano-Suiza which, in the early thirties, supplanted H6 37.2 model. Although this model weighed three tons, its pushrod ohv engine moved it along at 110 mph. It is said to have been most expensive car ever built (with Bugatti Royale); $40,000 got you one in U.S.*

BELOW LEFT: *Starkly simple instrument panel of 1912 Alfonso XIII Hispano-Suiza.* BELOW RIGHT: *Alfonso Hispano's 3-litre four-cylinder T-head engine had an exceptionally long stroke—180-mm compared to its 80-mm bore.*

ABOVE LEFT: *Beautifully simple engine of the 45-hp Boulogne Hispano. Removable lower half of carburetor allowed float chamber to be taken off for cleaning.*
ABOVE RIGHT: *Big V-12 engine of post-1931 Hispano-Suiza.*

Automoviles la Hispano-Suiza. Birkigt was an authentic genius and, strangely, like Henry Royce and W. O. Bentley, had been involved with railroad locomotives—Birkigt's, however, were electric instead of steam. Young Birkigt had a head-full of ideas which were to become current only many years later: the T-head engine with cylinders cast *en bloc,* shaft drive with torque taken by the rear springs (later credited to Hotchkiss), and as early as 1906, hollow, water-cooled brake shoes. In 1912 one of his racing cars even had a pump-type supercharger whose piston not only forced in mixture to the cylinders but also scavenged the burnt gases.

The Hispano-Suiza first made its mark in racing in 1910. In those days of giant-engined racing machines, there were also races for smaller lighter cars, *voiturettes.* Many of these, due to capacity regulations, had ridiculously tall single-cylinder engines. A 1910 Lion-Peugeot engine, for example, had an 80-mm bore and a 280-mm stroke—over eleven inches! Hispano, however, won the 1910 Coupe des Voiturettes with a four-cylinder-engined car driven by Zucarelli, the first time a car with such an engine had won it.

Proud of the Iberian victory, Alfonso XIII, the Bourbon king of Spain, immediately wanted such a car for his own use on the road. The factory not only obliged him but brought out a car, the T-15, which was named the Alfonso XIII in his honor (a perhaps dubious honor for a very fine automobile). If the term "sports car" had been current in 1912, that's what they'd have called the Alfonso. Fast for its time—about 75 mph—with good handling and acceleration and a distinctive musical note from its tailpipe, it was very much like its American contemporary, the Mercer Raceabout. In fact, it even had a T-head, four-cylinder engine, but with a rather extreme bore-stroke ratio—80 x 180 mm. The Alfonso model was made in the Barcelona factory as late as 1920, but was superseded by the big 37.2 Hispano.

In 1931 Hispano-Suiza took over the Ballot Company and the 37.2 and 45-Boulogne Hispanos gave way to an entirely different kind of beast—a quieter, plushier, and, to my mind, duller luxury apparatus, the V-12 Type 68. Shamefully, it now had its valves worked by lowly pushrods. The first of these pantechnicons had 9427-cc engines and had an exactly square bore-stroke, 100 mm x 100 mm. A later version with a 120-mm stroke had an engine with 11,300 cc—Birkigt used similar ones in railcars. These three-ton giants were no slouches, and it's no wonder, considering the size of their engines. They'd do 110 mph and go from 0 to 60 in 12 seconds, all without exceeding 3000 rpm. Like the earlier Hispanos they had servo-brakes, which they certainly needed.

There was also in 1933 a lesser, six-cylinder, 5-litre pushrod job, very posh but rather boring, which was turned out in the French factory. The Barcelona works built a smaller but similar 3-litre machine.

The French factory stopped building cars in 1939, but Barcelona persevered with its 3-litre cars until 1943. During the early fifties the Barcelona plant, which by then was part of the Empresa Nacional de Autocamiones and was engaged in building Enasa buses, came to life again with a most exciting sports car, the Pegaso. Somehow it failed to catch on. But I'll wager that if there had been some way to hang the magic Hispano-Suiza name on it, we'd see it still, giving the Ferraris a hard time.

53

Alfa Romeo Ask any hundred dedicated worshippers of the vintage sports car which of all such machines is their god and ninety-five of them, their nostrils aquiver, will bark, "Bugatti!" I, too, bend my knee to the Bugatti; there have never been more exciting cars to drive (when they were running right) or more breathtaking cars to look at, either bit by sculptured bit or as a whole. But I submit that there is one car which should stand up there with the Bugatti—the Alfa Romeo.

Certainly, the Alfa was not the product of a singular genius like Ettore Bugatti, whose workshops did things as he ordered them to and whose factory was his private and personal domain. It was the other way round at the Alfa Romeo factory—the designers were employees. But, although they could not indulge in the flights of inspired fancy of M. Bugatti, they still must have had great freedom, for the Alfa Romeo was hardly the sort of machine to which committees give birth.

On the contrary, it was a unique motorcar which in some important ways surpassed the revered Bugatti. Alfas, in my view, were pleasanter and easier to drive than most Bugattis. Excepting perhaps those least Bugatti-ish of all Bugattis, the Types 57. Alfas steered more easily and shifted with less noise once you got the hang of their crash gearboxes (Bugatti clutches *did* often stubbornly fail to let go their grip on their engines, resulting in painful grinding sounds).

Further, you could get all dressed up and go someplace in an Alfa with a reasonable chance that you'd arrive, perhaps windblown, but at least clean. The Bugattis I owned in the thirties often had me looking like a careless garage hand before I arrived at my destination. I always expected to fuss

with the machinery even if it was merely to sit on the side of the road cleaning red-hot spark plugs. And in winter—the cold, wet winter of our Northeast—every Alfa I ever owned (except for a newish one of the 60's which I now drive) started instantly—after tickling the carburetor—even after inactive weeks in a frigid garage.

Try starting, say, a Type 43, some morning in February (unless you've kept it warm and cozy in a nicely heated garage, as the imperious M. Bugatti suggested when a diffident customer brashly mentioned hard starting).

Although the Alfa Romeo factory had been building motorcars since 1909—first as A.L.F.A. (Anonima Lombarda Fabbrica Automobili)—it didn't reach its full stride as a builder of great sports cars—the 1750's, the 2.3's, and the 2.9's—until almost the 1930's.

Alfa Romeo had had considerable racing success long before that, notably with the Grand Prix P2's of 1924 and with specially prepared versions of its touring models in sports-car racing. Its first really sporting car (the 22/90 RLSS) did not, however, appear until 1925. In 1932, starry-eyed over the name "Alfa Romeo," which was winning everything in sight on the European Grand Prix circuits, I bought one of these RLSS machines—a much-used one which gave me great pleasure.

This 22/90 RLSS was a big, 129-inch wheelbase, black, five-passenger tourer with a 3-litre, six-cylinder, pushrod overhead valve engine. Its stroke was 110 mm, its bore 75 mm, and remarkable for its time, it had dry sump lubrication. Two carburetors were fitted. Originally they were Zeniths (some models had Solexes), but the previous owner had installed American Winfields. This en-

56

PRECEDING PAGES: *2.3-litre 1931 Alfa Romeo. Le Mans cars, such as this example is said to be, were required to have room for four passengers. They were also required to run for several laps with tops erected. Fenders on this car are not original.*

gine developed about 85 horsepower at 3600 rpm. The chassis frame was quite conventional, with semielliptic springs and four Hartford-type friction shock absorbers.

Compared to Alfa Romeos of but a few years later, the 22/90 was a rather clumsy, truck-like brute—not unlike the Bentleys or Mercedes' of its day. But compared to the dismal American models which were its contemporaries, it was a revelation of how much better cars could be. Even in the 1932-1936 period, during which time I owned the 22/90, its road holding, steering (two turns lock to lock), and visibility were far better than any Detroit car you could buy—and I include Packard, Lincoln, Cord, and Duesenberg. The Alfa's top speed of 85 (I got 88 once) was better than most in 1925, too.

The 22/90 had its faults. Its four-speed gearbox was a tooth-gnashing crash box. And its ratios were designed for Italians who drove mostly on corkscrewing mountain roads, seldom getting into fourth speed. Fourth was a slightly too high ratio, third was rather too low, so that downshifting to accelerate was impractical.

By today's standards, the 22/90's brakes would be considered pretty awful. In February, 1927, when the English "Motor" tested a 22/90, they thought them "remarkably efficient." I don't remember them with such enthusiasm. They were, of course, mechanical brakes. But instead of cables or rods, steel tapes linked the foot pedal with the wheels. Had these tapes gone directly to the wheels, retardation might have been better. But in 1925, front-wheel brakes were still in their childhood. The Alfa designers arranged the tapes to pull bits of chain over sprockets under the kingpins. These chains then pulled cables through holes bored in the kingpins, which cables then pulled levers

to apply the brakes if you hadn't had your collision by then. On early models the brake linings were of cast iron which squealed loudly enough to warn people that you were at least making an effort to stop—that is, unless you had first deafened them with your open-exhaust cutout. The cutout on the 22/90 RLSS I owned didn't merely allow the unmuffled exhaust gases out, it led them first through a long metal megaphone which amplified their fine big sound.

The 22/90 was eccentric in other ways. The clutch throwout bearing, for example, could be lubricated only by unbolting a cover in the clutch housing and applying grease with a brush! The overhead valve gear was lubricated by squirting a mixture of oil and kerosene over it.

The RLSS was a more sporting version of the RLS and RL models ("SS" for Super-Sport, "S" for Sport) and, unlike them, had a dash-mounted oil tank for its dry sump system. However, it still retained the crankcase oil filler of the RL and RLS types. The RL and RLS models also boasted a torque member—a steel arm alongside the drive shaft. This was eliminated in the RLSS models but its vestigial anchorages remained. One day I hit a hard bump while driving on New York's West Side and thought I heard a clank of metal. Arriving home I examined the underside of the car for damage, saw the empty anchorages and studied the Alfa instruction book illustrations to check on what was missing. The chassis photographs in the book were for all three models and showed the torque arm. I frantically drove back to where I'd had my bump to look for the torque arm. There was, of course, no sign of it. I stopped garbage trucks, police cars, road sweepers, taxi drivers, and asked them if they'd picked up

a such-and-such shaped piece of steel. No luck. I was desolated. Only after I had written the factory ordering a new torque arm did I find out that my 22/90 never had one.

The RLSS 22/90 was murderous to drive in hot weather. The foot board of thick aluminum got hot enough to melt the rubber soles of my shoes. This, coupled with the tank full of hot oil over the driver's knees, made the cockpit as uncomfortable as a steam bath. This warmth was added to the hard work of shifting gears and the tramping on the heavy multiplate clutch. After a summer trip, I looked as if I'd just finished a hard day's work in a boiler room.

Special TF (for Targa Florio) models derived from the RLSS 22/90's made Alfas famous in the Targa Florio, that still-tough race over the Sicilian mountains. Some of these TF's had 3-litre engines like the RLSS's (2994 cc) but others had 3620-cc engines which pushed out more horsepower and more speed—125 bhp and 95 miles per hour. All the TF's had seven main bearing engines, too; the normal 22/90 engines had only four mains.

One of these 3.6-litre TF's, driven by Ugo Sivocci, won the Targa in 1923. A 3-litre-engined TF driven by Antonio Ascari came in second.

In 1927, Alfa Romeo's racing-car engineer, the great Vittorio Jano, took the Alfa sports car down a new, more logical path. From now on the cars were designed from scratch as sports cars. They were no longer merely super-tuned versions of the factory's bread-and-butter touring machines.

The new cars were light, small, nimble machines, direct descendants of the P2 Grand Prix racers. As far back as 1925 a few 1500-cc single-overhead-camshaft, six-cylinder-engined cars had been made. These machines, however, had a rather mediocre performance (65 mph) and were but a prelude to the first of the line of hemispherically combustion-chambered, twin-overhead-camshaft-engined machines that for the next decade would make Alfa Romeo one of the great sports-car names of all time.

In 1928 a supercharged, six-cylinder, 1500-cc version, with its engine moved rearward to accommodate a crankshaft-driven Roots supercharger, won the Italian Mille Miglia. Ramponi and Campari (of the aperitif-making Campari family) drove it. At the Shelsley Walsh Hillclimb in England a blown six-cylinder 1500 made fastest sports-car time of the day. And at Boulogne a Czarist named Ivanowski walked away with the Georges Boillot Cup for first place—I could go on and on. Anyhow, that was quite a season for a sports car making its debut.

But Alfa wasn't standing still. In 1929, what I still consider the greatest Alfa of them all—the six-cylinder 1750—was born. It still had the 88-mm stroke of the 1500, but its cylinder bore was now 65 mm, which gave it its extra 250 cc.

I bought one of these early 1750's in 1936 from an enthusiastic young Florentine named Giuseppe Fantacci. Mechanically the car was fine, except that Fantacci's girl friend had thought the suspension too hard. To please her Fantacci had removed all four shock absorbers. When I first saw the car in a garage near Washington Square in Greenwich Village, it looked tired. Its grey paint had gone chalky, the upholstery was tatty.

I had the car painted Alfa red (of course), replaced the upholstery, found a new set of friction shockers, and had the engine tuned. When I went with my brother to collect the newly restored vehicle at Zumbach's I was stunned. The car looked and sounded new.

Further aspects of 2.3-litre Le Mans Alfa Romeo.
Car similar to this, driven by Britishers Sir Henry Birkin
and Lord Howe, won that 24-hour race
in 1931 at an average speed of 78.13 mph. Fussy cover over
quickly needed spare tire is recent addition.

But I hadn't reckoned with Fantacci. Before I could climb aboard to try my new jewel, Fantacci had vaulted into one seat, my brother into the other, and off they screamed down the street. It seemed hours before they returned. My brother was speechless with delight—he couldn't tell me until later about Fantacci's frightening virtuoso exploits. Fantacci kept repeating, "My macchina—b-*yoot*iful—b-*yoot*iful."

They were right. That 1750 handled like nothing I had ever driven. It was not the hottest Alfa of the line—that model had a blower and was called the Super-Sport con Compressore; my car was the Super-Sport *senza* Compressore (without blower). There were also a less-sporting model called simply Sport and various other touring models of the 1750. In these cars the engine sat right behind the radiator. But in my Super Sport sans blower the engine was placed as far back as that in the supercharged job, leaving a lot of empty space in front which contained only a polished steel tube for the long hand crank. It always seemed to me that this first unblown Alfa I owned handled better than some of my later 1750's which had superchargers. Perhaps the blower out front did something to the weight distribution.

The last of the 1750's—the supercharged, six-cylinder 1750 Gran Sport—was the greatest of all. The quickest way to tell a Gran Sport from the earlier Super Sport is to look at the supercharger. The Super Sport Memini carburetor is on the right; the intake manifold (the most beautiful one ever made) to the engine crosses over the top of the blower. The Gran Sport carburetor is on the left side of the engine, eliminating the crossover.

The later six-cylinder 1750 Gran Sport models were capable of 105 miles per hour.

Their engines put out about 100 horsepower. A vertical shaft at the rear drove the twin-overhead camshafts. Compression was only 5.25 to 1 (it was 6.25 to 1 in the unblown models). The Roots-type blower compressed the charge of gas and air at about six pounds per square inch and it was necessary to add oil to the fuel for its lubrication. A tecalemit fitting on the casing provided grease for the blower gears. On early models you had to remove the front of the casing to smear the gears with vaseline.

Nowadays on twin-overhead-cam engines like Jaguars or modern Alfas, it's a fussy and expensive chore to adjust valve clearances. You have to remove the camshafts and change shims or valve caps. But the Alfas of the thirties used a lovely and ingenious method for the job. (Hispano-Suiza used a similar system.) All you had to do to adjust the valves of an Alfa was to set the end of a little tool (provided with each car) into a socket cast into the head. The tool had a toothed sector which meshed with gear teeth cut into mushroom-shaped discs which acted as valve tappets and which were screwed into the ends of the valves. Each valve had two discs—one for adjustment, the other to lock it. To adjust a valve you merely twisted the tool.

The 1750 Alfas had other pleasurable conveniences. When you removed the filler cap to add oil to the crankcase, it exposed a hole lower down which prevented overfilling. If you poured in too much oil, the excess ran out onto the ground. Nor did 1750s have anything so crude as a dipstick for measuring the oil level. A float in the crankcase raised and lowered a brass rod which slid in a groove cast into the side of the crankcase. You didn't even have to raise the hood to check the oil—one of the hood louvers was

TOP: 1910 *A.L.F.A.; Romeo wasn't part of the name until* 1918.
CENTER: TF *(Targa Florio) version of standard RLSS 22/90 sports car. This road-racing machine differed from standard RLSS 22/90's in having seven- rather than four-main-bearing crankshaft.* BOTTOM: *Boat-tailed 22/90 3-litre overhead-valve sports Alfa of mid-twenties, capable of 85 mph.*

RIGHT: *Almost every sports car Alfa Romeo built had an engine which descended from that in this eight-cylinder twin-overhead-camshaft 2-litre Grand Prix car, the P2 of 1924. That year it won the Italian and European Grands Prix.*
BELOW: *Campari driving winning supercharged 1500-cc Alfa Romeo over Raticosa Pass during 1928 Mille Miglia.*
BOTTOM LEFT: *Campari again, with Ramponi in 1750-cc Alfa Romeo which won 1929 Mille Miglia.*
BOTTOM RIGHT: *2.3 Alfa driven.by Bonini in 1931 Mille Miglia.*

cut wide enough so you could look at the oil-level rod through it. This rod on the side of the engine wasn't the only oil-level indicator on the car. Another one rose and fell to indicate the amount of oil in an auxiliary oil tank inside the cockpit. The contents of this small, flat tank could be let into the engine by means of a valve when the oil-pressure gauge on the dash gave warning. People were always fiddling with this valve on my first 1750 and I put a lock on it after someone (unbeknownst to me) let all the auxiliary oil tank flow into the already full crankcase. Although I made a smoke screen which filled a canyon-like New York street from wall to wall, I didn't foul a plug.

The 1750 Alfa had a quite conventional 109-inch chassis with a half-elliptic spring at each corner, controlled by Hartford-type friction shock absorbers. Brakes were mechanically operated by rods with a rather tricky adjustment system. The early 1750's clutch was a multiplate affair of miniscule dimensions and grew only slightly larger on later models. This multiplate clutch was the only thing that ever gave me any trouble— and that was through my own ineptitude. I let my Alfa get stuck in sand and in my clumsy efforts to extricate myself, overheated and warped some of the clutch's steel plates. Even with a solidly locked, nonreleasable clutch, however, I was able to work my way home by switching off every time I stopped. Shifting gears on a 1750's nonsynchro box was perfectly feasible, if nerve-wracking, clutch or no clutch.

Although its mechanism is a joy to examine, the just-right architecture of its two-seater Zagato body more than satisfying to contemplate, there seldom was a more exciting yet safe-feeling car to drive than a 1750 Alfa. I never went to take mine out of its

garage without a pleasurably nervous feeling that I was embarking on an adventure.

If the car had not been used for a while, it was the usual drill to lift the hood and jiggle the pin on the float chamber of the carburetor to flood it. After that you took your seat, pushed the ignition light in—it was also the starter button—and scared the daylights out of any new passenger. For Alfas exploded into action. One moment there would be quiet and the next you'd be engulfed in sudden violent sound. And if you paid attention to the instruction book, you kept on making this mechanical bedlam at 1000 rpm for ten minutes before taking to the road.

Once under way, accompanied by the delightful right-sounding uproar from its gears, its blower, its valves, and the usual whew-p, whew-p of its exhaust, you were the happiest man on the road. The Alfa did *exactly* what you wanted it to. A touch on the centrally mounted gas pedal and the revs scream up— *right now!* You had but to communicate your thoughts about your course—almost telepathically—to the steering wheel and the car pointed there. A flick of the wrist and you were around corners—flat and fast. But you could not be ham-handed. Should you grip the wheel hard to prevent its slight jiggling on road irregularities, you would be all over the highway.

The 1750 Alfas had a fine record in competition. In the Italian Mille Miglia of 1929 —first and third. In 1929, too, first, second, and third in the touring (sports) car category in the Belgian G.P. at Spa. In the tourist trophy race in Ireland, Nuvolari, Campari, and Varzi took first, second, and third as rain poured down. Malcolm Campbell in a saurian-sized brute of a 38/250 Mercedes-Benz was one mile an hour faster than Nuvolari's winning speed of 70.88 mph, but lost on handicap.

The 1750 Gran Sport Alfas cost circa $7,000 in the early thirties.

In the grim depression year of 1931 few manufacturers of precision motorcars brought out entirely new models—but Alfa Romeo didn't have their worries. Alfa had Mussolini. Il Duce needed Alfa to give fascism at least *some* glory, so Alfa got Italian government lire, plus a modicum of government control, which it still has.

The new Alfa was the eight-cylinder 2300 —the great 2.3. Although at first glance it looked not unlike a slightly larger 1750 (which was made until 1934), raising the hood revealed it to be entirely different. Now it had a straight-eight blown engine with its blower alongside instead of out front. Its cylinder dimensions were still those of the 1750's—65 by 88 mm. But now the cylinders were cast in two blocks of four, which permitted the space between them to accommodate the gears which drove the camshafts and the supercharger. One long, light-alloy cylinder head covered all eight cylinders. The ten-main-bearing crankshaft was split midway by the camshaft and blower gears. Early models of the 2.3 had cast-iron blocks; later ones were cast of light alloy. All had cylinder liners. And the 2.3's, unlike the 1750's, were given dry sump lubrication by Signor Jano. A "normal" 2.3's engine pushed out some 140 horsepower at 4900 rpm, but few 2.3's were normal. Some were bored out to 2.6 litres and put out 165 bhp.

You had to be careful on a 2.3 not to run with a weak mixture. If you did, cracks might appear between the spark-plug hole and the exhaust-valve seat—a problem you never had on a 1750. The chassis of the 2.3 was not unlike that of the 1750, except that the rear semielliptic springs were mounted outboard of the chassis. Further, the rear friction shocks were adjustable from the cockpit. The biggest difference was in the brakes. These were huge—with a 15¾-inch internal diameter—and completely filled the wire wheels. And you needed good brakes, for a standard 2.3 was capable of 115 mph.

Until recently a friend of mine, Ed Bond, of Old Saybrook, Connecticut, owned a 2.6 version and occasionally, with some qualms, he let me drive it. It was much like a 1750, but with less delicacy of feel, and the increase of 850 cc made it perform more vigorously. Its instruments, like those of a 1750, were hidden under its cowl. But Bond's had a big rev-counter mounted on the steering column, so that you didn't sound the horn with your chin every time you ducked down to see how fast you were going. Seating was like that in a 1750, too—too narrow and high, so that the top of your head was above the top of the windshield.

But it *went!*

This Alfa was clocked at 121 mph at Brooklands Track in England when it was the property of Guy Templar. And it can still make it to 60 in 10 seconds. Although Zagato bodies were more common, this one's coachwork was by Castagna. With either body such an Alfa cost about $9,000 more than thirty years ago.

Alfa Romeos in the early thirties were the kings of Grand Prix racing. They had overwhelmed the Bugattis, and the Third Reich's Mercedes-Benz's and Auto-Unions had not yet, in turn, beaten them. And they continued to lead in sports-car racing. Driven by the British milords Howe and Birkin they won at Le Mans in 1931. They took the first three places in the 1932 Mille Miglia (with two 2.3's and a 1750) and in 1933 they were

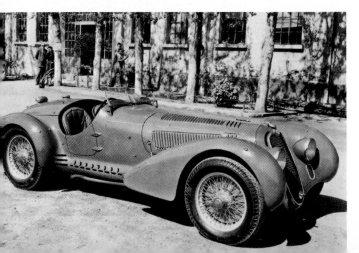

TOP: *Nuvolari at the wheel of the 2.3-litre
Monza Alfa Romeo which won the 1931 Targa Florio.*
ABOVE LEFT: *Compare businesslike look of
this 2.3 Alfa with gussied-up collector's car on pages 54-55.
Cortese and Guidotti brought this car into
second place in 1932 Le Mans 24-hour race.* ABOVE: *Quickest
way to tell a 1750 cc from a 2.3 Alfa is to look at the
brake drums. The 2.3's, as this one, have bigger
wheel-filling brake drums.* LEFT: *The 8C 2900B appeared in
1937, had independent front suspension.*

TOP LEFT: *Closed version of the 8C 2900B.* TOP RIGHT: *1929 1750-cc*
Super-Sport senza Compressore which had room for supercharger but no supercharger.
Fenders are replacements. ABOVE: *Twin-overhead-camshaft engine of*
blown Gran Sport 1750-cc Alfa Romeo. Supercharger is at lower right. Note voluminous
instructions engraved on plate fastened to camshaft cover.

*Blown 2.3 Alfa Romeo convertibles
were rare. With top up and windows closed, the
uproar was more than most people
could stand. Hard springing was ruination
of such fancy coachwork as this.*

one, two, three at Le Mans. In fact, their repeated victories at Le Mans and in the Mille Miglia became almost boring.

As the thirties waned, the 2.3 Alfas with their solid front axles and mechanical brakes were beginning to be thought a mite old-fashioned. A new Alfa was being born.

This was the eight-cylinder 2900B which appeared in 1937. Vittorio Jano, it is said, decided to build his new model around some thirty 2.9 engines which had been originally destined for Grand Prix cars, but which were now superseded by twelve-cylinder G.P. engines.

The 2900B's were independently suspended all around and could be had in two chassis lengths—the 108-inch Corto or the 118-inch Lungo. Their 68 x 100 mm engines put out 180 horsepower, had twin superchargers with Weber carburetors, and used the same two-banks-of-four-cylinders arrangement as the 2.3's. A speed of 125 mph was possible and 0 to 60 in under nine seconds. Brakes were now hydraulically operated, but the clutch was still a multi-plate device.

The first 2900B I saw was imported by Maclure Halley, a leading habitué of Zumbach's. His prize after a long wait, including a trip to Milan to hurry things up, arrived in New York just before World War II. To me, this Alfa looked too big, too plushy, too civilized. It did not have that lean old Spartan look, and I feared it had also lost that hard, nervous feel Alfas ought to have.

But I was wrong. After Halley took me through Central Park I knew it was a real Alfa all right—vicious, and with that old, hard Alfa sound. And although it didn't quite have that quick flick-of-the-wrist steering, it handled beautifully..

And the eight-cylinder 2900B proved it had the stuff in sports racing, too. In the 1938 Mille Miglia it was one, two, and three again—Biondetti averaging a shattering 84.13 miles an hour for a thousand miles.

Alfa now exports a fine line of medium-priced cars into this country: the 1600-cc, twin-camshaft Duetto two-seater, which I consider the best sports car in its class; the 1600 Giulia GT Veloce, the 115-mph, grand-touring version of the Duetto; and the slightly less puissant Giulia Super, which still reaches 110 mph from 1600 cc.

RIGHT: *Super-civilized six-cylinder 2600-cc Spyder. This is 1966 twin-cam Alfa.*

BELOW: *Beloved four-cylinder 1300-cc Giuliettas and 1600-cc Giulias were best-handling small sports cars (except perhaps Lotus Elan) in recent years.*

BOTTOM: *1967 1600-cc Alfa Romeo Duetto is modernized Giulia roadster, with five-speed gearbox, 115-mph speed.*

69

PRECEDING PAGES: 1914 *Prince Henry*
Vauxhall was one of the world's first sports cars.
It had a 75-hp 4-litre engine.
Note that radiator is well-forward — an
unusual placement in an early car.

A. J. Hancock on a 1914 racing Vauxhall.
It had a twin-overhead-camshaft 4½-litre 130-hp
engine which revved at over 4000 rpm,
remarkably high for its day. The mechanic seems to
be warming his arm on the exhaust pipe.

vauxhall There were two great Vauxhalls: the Prince Henry of pre-World War I days and the O.E. 30-98 of the twenties. The first Vauxhall of which I had any experience was the 30-98, in the thirties. It wasn't until many years later that I was able to examine and ride in a Prince Henry. In the interest of logical chronology, however, I'll take the Prince Henry first.

The Prince Henry Vauxhall got its name from the famous Prinz Heinrich von Preussen "Tours"—high-speed rallies of a sort—which started in 1908 in Germany. In 1910 Vauxhall Motors entered a 3-litre machine. Although it did not win (a Porsche-designed Austro-Daimler did), it was the prototype of a later 4-litre type which was called a Prince Henry, although it never ran in the Prince Henry trials.

The Prince Henry I got to know, fleetingly, was the prized possession of the late Laurence Pomeroy, that most literate of motoring writers. He was, I suppose, especially enamored of his car since his father had designed it. I first saw him driving his lovely machine on the track at Thompson, Connecticut, during the British-American vintage-car rally in 1957. "Pom" was a first-class driver and it was really something to see him charging around at full bore on the banking in the high, narrow, and softly sprung, tubby-looking Prince Henry. A few years later, in England, Pomeroy took me for a ride, a shattering experience.

You'd expect a man to drive a pre-World War I touring car with gingerly respect. Not Pomeroy. He charged off into thick London traffic as if he were behind the wheel of a Ferrari. When we took our first roundabout (traffic circle in American) at 40 or so, I was ready to abandon ship. But the Prince Henry, although it leaned a bit on its soft springs, treated the corner disdainfully—as if it didn't exist. Nor did Pomeroy seem to use any steering effort going around. This delicacy of handling is due largely to the low, unsprung weight of the Prince Henry. Its light wheels, thin, light tires, and lack of front-wheel brakes all help.

Once we reached open country I was aware of another delightful characteristic of the Prince Henry: the effortless way it ate up the miles. With its 3-to-1 rear-end ratio, its 4-litre engine was only turning over 2000 rpm at 60 mph and the four-cylinder 75-hp engine, if not absolutely quiet, was remarkably smooth at that speed. Its top speed was 75 mph—fast for 1914. At 60 you just loaf along.

When Pomeroy lifted the hood to show me the engine, I must admit that I was somewhat disappointed. It was a most dismal-looking side-valve mechanism almost lost in the vast under-hood space.

As we further examined the Prince Henry, I was particularly surprised at the small size of the rear brake drums. (There were, of course, no front-wheel brakes.) "Pom" explained that these were controlled by the outside hand-brake lever, that another more powerful retarder worked on the rear of the excellent four-speed gearbox, but that he used it only in dire circumstances, since it became extremely hot and required frequent adjustment—every few hundred miles if used often. Still, I hadn't noticed any alarums due to poor braking. As Pomeroy said, "In heavy traffic I drive as if I have *no* brakes."

Many people consider the Prince Henry the first British sports car, and I agree. In fact, many of the other cars developed from the Prince Henry trials were of that new breed, the sports car, although the term "sports car" wouldn't become usage until the twenties. And the Prince Henry acquitted itself very well in competition. In 1913 it took twenty-three first places at Brooklands Track and, in addition, won no less than thirty-five hill climbs.

By 1913, however, there already existed what were really the first few of those great sports cars—the 30-98's. These were the early E types—but they weren't called that until they went into production after the war in 1919. They had larger engines than the Prince Henrys, being bored out to 98-mm, compared to the Prince Henry's 95-mm, and their crankshafts had a longer throw—75 instead of 70 mm, which gave them a 150-mm stroke (the shafts were stretched cold!). Only six cars were built prewar.

In 1919 these cars, with their fixed-head, single-carburetor (Zenith), side-valve engines, at last appeared under their new and later famous name—the E type Velox 30-98. Thirty because its rated R.A.C. horsepower had gone up from the Prince Henry's 25, and 98 because that was its actual power output. Laurence Pomeroy, Sr., had wanted to replace the old engine with a new overhead-camshaft design, but the timid, money-conscious directors of the company prevented this, causing Pomeroy to leave and go to the U.S.A. Here he designed an advanced, all-aluminum car for Alcoa, which was also the victim of another fearful group of company directors.

The E type 30-98 was a most pleasant motorcar with much of the charm of the Prince Henry, but it was the later O.E., with its pushrod, overhead-valve engine, which became the truly great sports car of the twenties.

Although the O.E. appeared in 1923, I didn't see one until 1931 when production had already been stopped for almost four years. At that time there existed in New York a most wonderful emporium for the sale of used foreign cars, mostly sports cars. This occupied a dim and dusty upper floor of the Liberty Storage warehouse and was presided over by a lovable gentleman named Ray Gilhooley. (His name is still used at Indianapolis to describe a certain type of spectacular spinout, which he first performed in an Isotta-Fraschini in about 1913—almost killing himself in the process.) Although Mr. Gilhooley was ostensibly engaged in the business of selling cars, it always seemed to me that what he enjoyed most was taking tyros like me out into the heavy New York traffic and frightening the daylights out of us. We must have enjoyed it because almost every Saturday morning my brother and I showed up to take a ride in one of Gilhooley's latest acquisitions.

That particular Saturday morning it was an O.E. 30-98 with a bright aluminum roadster body. We were suitably frightened, but we were charmed, too. The Vauxhall handled and went like nothing we'd ever been in until then—it should have since it put out some 120 horsepower and the body weighed very little.

It made a lovely deep noise, had a beautifully handling gearbox, steered impeccably but a bit heavily since it took but one turn lock to lock, and had as smoothly running an engine as I'd ever tried. (Ray let me drive it once he realized that I might, in my enthusiasm, actually buy this one.) Two things put me off. First the price: Gilhooley wanted $150 *plus* my near-new Model A Ford. Secondly, the brakes were poor, even for 1931.

Although Gilhooley said the brakes merely required adjusting, I found out later that the 30-98's brakes were notorious for lack of stopping power, even though they were by

74

ABOVE: *A 1909 Vauxhall.*
BELOW: *Famous O.E. 30-98 Vauxhall. The 4½-litre*
O.E. 30-98 first appeared in 1923. Bentley
fanciers and Vauxhall enthusiasts have long engaged in the same
kind of controversy as Mercer and Stutz adherents.

ABOVE: *1914 racing Vauxhall in Tourist Trophy Race.*

TOP LEFT: *Clean 4½-litre overhead-valve engine of the O.E. 30-98 Vauxhall.*

MIDDLE LEFT: *The late Laurence Pomeroy Jr. with his Prince Henry Vauxhall. Note extreme front-wheel lock.*

BOTTOM LEFT: *View of O.E. 30-98 showing famous "kidney box" through which front-wheel brakes were actuated.*

then on all four wheels. Operated by cables and rods from a kidney-shaped box hung on a cross member between the front goosenecks, they were bad enough to inspire the instruction-book writer to say, "should it become necessary to check the car's progress, the handbrake is the correct brake to use, the foot-operated brake being in reserve for emergency." I wonder what Ralph Nader would say about *that?*

Later 30-98's had a primitive type of hydraulic brakes.

The Gilhooley 30-98, which I turned down, was bought by a young man who thought it needed restoration. To which end he completely dismantled it. I remember seeing its fluted radiator leaning against a wall of a garage, its engine parts in boxes. For years it gathered dust this way. Happily, a few years ago, after the young chap's death in a too exuberantly driven Lancia, the parts were bought by an optimistic enthusiast and the *30-98* is on the road again.

Vauxhall still builds cars of a sort, but nothing like the glorious 30-98. After all, General Motors has owned the name since 1926.

Rolls-Royce

PRECEDING PAGES: *1910 40/50-hp Silver Ghost Rolls-Royce. Ghost was built from 1907 until 1925. Only the Model T Ford had as long a life.*

ABOVE: *Charles S. Rolls and fancy friends in 1905. Rolls is in front seat wearing top hat. Car is unsuccessful 30-hp Six.*

RIGHT: *Rolls-Royce four-cylinder Light Twenties in the 1906 Tourist Trophy Race. No. 4, in front, won the race.*

BELOW LEFT: *Two-cylinder engine of the 10-hp 1905 Rolls-Royce.*

BELOW RIGHT: *10-hp Rolls-Royce, built from 1904 to 1906, was first production car.*

Rolls-Royce Get a powerful idea into people's heads, even for a short time, and they and their children and their children's children will go on believing it almost forever, it seems. The Rolls-Royce is a classic example of such unquestioning belief: an astonishing number of people still regard it as "the Best Car In the World." In my opinion there is little doubt that from 1907 until the start of the Great War in 1914, the Rolls-Royce deserved that grandiose description.

Since that meeting of brass hats in the railway carriage at Compiègne on November 11, 1918, however, other great machines have come along. The Royce, although still a truly superb car, can't be called "Best." For many years now it has been *one* of the best.

But during the first seven years or so of its existence, the Rolls-Royce Silver Ghost was so far superior to any machine then on earth (except perhaps in speed, which to Henry Royce was a somewhat secondary consideration) that it is hard to pick the car which stood second to it.

What did the Silver Ghost have? Why was it the king of motorcars?

First, it was silky smooth, quieter perhaps than any car ever built, quieter even than any Rolls-Royce up to the present day. And such an oily hush in a rapidly rotating and sliding assemblage of engine parts is not achieved by happenstance. The six-cylinder Ghost engine was the result of an infinite refinement of workmanship, of endless experimenting, of superlative materials—although I must admit, too, that some of its silence (and longevity) was to no little extent due to the fact that it was understressed (and over-muffled). Much more power could have been got out of it but wasn't because its small carburetor throat and small intake valves made for in-built throttling.

Nor did the engine suffer from the lubrication problems of most others of its day. It dispensed with the usual external total-loss oil pumps, which either over-oiled or under-oiled the bearings and cylinders in their care. Most drivers cautiously set the drip feeds of such primitive oilers generously open, and cars signaled their departure with a white cloud of oily smoke. But not a Ghost. For Ghosts had hollow crankshafts lubricated from an *internal* oil pump, which recirculated the oil after use, like high-speed steam engines of the period. Royce also provided a neat contrivance which supplied extra lubrication in times of stress. If you pushed the throttle down hard, a valve opened and sent along additional oil.

It was very hard—in fact, well-nigh impossible—to break up a Ghost chassis unless you rammed it into something like an abutment of the Firth of Forth bridge. But rough roads wouldn't budge a thing. Royce had already tried to make the chassis come unstuck before you got it by torturing its prototype on a rack of rollers called a "bumping machine." Royce's boys at the Derby factory did everything short of putting that chassis into an oversized iron maiden, or exploding a charge of gelignite under it. The Silver Ghosts' chassis were, in fact, so tough that they were able to bear up nobly under the almost four-ton weight of armored-car bodies and go into battle over the rocks and through the deserts of the Middle East during World War I. The only troubles they had were with tires punctured by Turkish bullets and with a spot of boiling when, buttoning up for action, the armored doors protecting the radiators were shut. Hub bearings, not designed for use under the prodigious weight of the tank-like carriage work, gave a bit of bother, too. After the war armored cars which were sent to the outer reaches of the Empire had heftier bearings fitted.

Longevity was always a strong point with Rolls-Royce, and I think it's pretty hard to beat the record set by those armored cars of the first great war. For twenty-odd years later some of them came out again to help subdue Hitler's Afrika Korps in the western desert.

This incredible durability of the Rolls-Royce Ghost chassis was due to Royce's unique methods of putting sections of metal together. A Royce frame, unlike those beneath other cars, was bolted, not riveted. Tapered, square-headed bolts were fitted exactly to hand-reamed, tapered holes without the least looseness or play.

For fastening other parts, say, components of the rear axle housing, Royce used many tiny bolts, their heads almost touching each other. In Royce's words, he "sewed" the parts together. There could be no leakage, no uneven strains. Where other car builders used ten bolts, Royce might use forty—which once made the mechanic engaged in dismantling a Rolls rear axle for me most unhappy and profane. I might add that this diddling with the differential proved quite unnecessary; the slight noise I thought it made was caused by the vibration of a hinged metal trapdoor, which the French body builder had arranged in order to provide access to the differential's oil filler. I should have known that Rolls-Royce differential gears just didn't make any noise.

In the days of the Silver Ghost, several cars were kept around the shop for the sole purpose of testing rear axles. When a rear end was built, it was installed in one of the test cars, run for fifty miles, taken apart and its teeth examined by a team of "dentists," who honed and scraped any rough spots.

After that it was run on a test bench and carefully listened to for noise. If at all noisy (by Royce standards), it came apart again and was again ministered to by the "dentists."

Royce had a thing about noise. Sometimes he seemed to go out of his way to design elements which in lesser cars would invite noise, but which in his cars would be silent. For example, the Ghost engine's valve mechanism—tappets, stems, guides, and springs—were nakedly exposed, which was pretty archaic even in 1907, but Royce stoutly insisted that other makers enclosed theirs because they were noisy and that his would be quiet without the muffling effect of enclosure.

Assume that it's 1911 and that you're the proud owner and driver of a 40/50 hp Silver Ghost touring car. What was it like to drive?

Your car is a recently announced new version of the Ghost—the London-Edinburgh type, based on the Rolls which has just run from London to Edinburgh in top gear only and then been timed at Brooklands Track at 78.26 mph. It is different from your old 1908 Rolls (which you traded in) in having cantilever rear springs, instead of platform springs, with a third spring lying crossways at the rear of the car. It has a three-speed gearbox, unlike your earlier machine which had four speeds, the highest being an overdrive. (Later Rolls would have four speeds again, but with a low first gear for starting on steep hills and with a fourth speed which was a direct drive.)

The 7½-litre engine with its cylinders in two banks of three is practically unchanged except for slightly higher compression—3.5 to 1 instead of 3.2 to 1, as in your old Rolls. The carburetor is slightly bigger, too.

Externally, the London-Edinburgh looks wonderfully different and more sporting. Its

82

Rear aspect of the 1910 40/50-hp six-cylinder Silver Ghost. Earlier Ghosts had a transverse platform rear spring, but this was eliminated by 1910. Note that the speedometer at far right has two dials, one for miles, the other for kilometers.

hood is tapered to a cowl, whereas the earlier Royce had a low, parallel-sided hood terminating in a flat dashboard. You sit lower now, and the long front fenders sweep backward in a light graceful curve.

As you walk admiringly around your car, you turn down its grease cups, turn the try cock to check if there is enough oil in the sump, and then set that delightful spark control on the steering column to "late." Rolls always were marked "early" and "late" instead of "advance" and "retard," as on ordinary cars.

You turn the switch on the steering-wheel hub and walk toward the front of the car, admiring the classic radiator for the hundredth time. Almost casually you flick the handcrank upwards just once and the engine is gently alive, running as lightly as a sewing machine. You let it warm for a few minutes.

As you climb into your seat, although you know the engine couldn't have stalled, you reassure yourself by a glance at the slightly flickering oil pressure gauge. Reaching down, you pull out the stick jammed between the bearing housing on the steering column and the clutch pedal, which has served to keep the conical clutch facings from sticking to each other overnight.

You press the clutch pedal in again, release the hand brake, and slip the nickel-plated gear lever—outside the body on the right—into first gear. Then you glide down the curving driveway, passing the gardener who respectfully pulls his forelock (remember, this is England in 1911). At the end of the driveway you stop and do something that, somehow, gives you inordinate pleasure every time you go driving in your Rolls. You set the governor on the top of the steering column. This precise device will keep the engine running at a set speed, up and down hill, no matter what the load (but at no more than half throttle), and allow you to make a smooth start from rest without touching the accelerator pedal. And you can make noiseless gear changes using it, not an easy accomplishment with the rather tricky gearbox on a Ghost—and on later Rolls, too. But after a mile or two of enjoying the precision of the governor, you move it toward the end of its quadrant, for you will not want it on today's fast run into the hills north of the border.

Once on the open road you give the great car its head. At 70 it moves with the slightest of fore-and-aft rocking motions, but silently, smoothly as a cloud. You pass through a crowded town; it's market day. As you manipulate your car's rather thick-rimmed handful of steering wheel to thread your way through the farmers' carts, there's no feeling of heaviness. You don't even shift gears, for the Rolls will throttle down to a walking pace in high gear. Then, as you leave the town, you accelerate smoothly, without a hint of hesitation, back up to your 70-mile cruising speed. The road becomes rougher, unpaved and lumpy, as you approach the hills to the north. But the Royce takes it in stride, softly rising and falling over the inequalities of the road, its steering steady. You are in the hills now. The road climbs through a series of acute, steep, hairpin bends. Before each hairpin you shift, double clutching, of course, and cramp the steering wheel hard over. The front wheels, unencumbered by brakes, lock over to an impossible angle and, throwing gravel, you're away on the upper arm of the hairpin. This in spite of your 135½-inch wheelbase, which in later front-wheel-braked cars might force you to reverse at each hairpin—to take it in two bites.

On the steep downgrades you control your

84

1913 London-Edinburgh Rolls-Royce. In 1911 a special Rolls with bigger carburetor and higher than standard compression (3½ to 1) went from London to Edinburgh in top gear only, then reached 78.26 mph in speed test. Similar cars, called London-Edinburgh models, were then made for sale.

speed with the hand brake. But although only fitted to the rear wheels (the foot brake works on the drive shaft), the car is held in check. (On the road at speed they stop well enough, too; there is no traffic to speak of in 1911.)

Back home again you check your gasoline mileage—twenty miles to the Imperial gallon—not bad. You're pleased at the economy, forgetting that you paid more than £1,500 ($7,500) for the Rolls, a tidy sum in 1911 and equal to $30,000 today.

It is hard to realize that Frederick·Henry Royce's first car of 1904 was a mere three years behind him when the Silver Ghost first came on the market and immediately took a place with the top marques of its day: Mercedes, Panhard, Napier, and Daimler.

Royce was no longer a young man when he built his first car. He was just past forty and had already spent many years—some of them very hard years, indeed—rising from poverty to considerable success in building Royce Limited, a manufactory of electric

Pride of Silver Ghosts in 1907. Silver Ghost was named after a six-cylinder 40/50-hp model which, for publicity purposes, was painted in silver, trimmed with nickel plate instead of usual brass. It still sits in RR's London showroom.

cranes and dynamos. Fascinated by the early motorcar and with enough money to indulge himself at last, he bought a small, used French Decauville at the urging of his business associates, who thought it would bolster his poor health. (Earlier he had been involved in a short romance with a De Dion quadricycle, a device like two bicycles side by side with a tiny single-cylindered engine mounted between the two rear wheels.)

For its day the noisy, vibrating Decauville was not too bad a machine, but Royce was sure he could build a better one. Further, Royce Ltd. was not doing so well as it might, and Royce had ideas about the company getting into the burgeoning new motorcar business.

So Royce went ahead and built three 10-hp, two-cylinder cars. There was nothing revolutionary about them, but they were built to standards of craftsmanship ingrained in Royce since his boyhood apprenticeship in the shops of the Great Northern Railway. Every bit of metal, every tiny process of machining, had to be of a quality previously unattained in the construction of motorcars. Royce, of course, did not build these first machines with his own two hands. He had in his factory perfectly good machinists already trained to his heartbreaking perfectionism. Some components, like cylinder castings, were made outside, as they are today, although there was a long period when Rolls-Royce cast its own. An example of Royce's insistence on perfection occurred at the time when the first Ghosts were under construction a few years later. A cylinder casting which had been supplied from outside burst while under test. Royce, furious, picked up a sledge hammer and smashed eleven similar castings which were already machined and ready for installation. No

further such castings were used until they were redesigned with strengthening ribs.

Royce's two-cylinder cars (they were ready on April 1, 1904) were all that he had expected: quiet, as vibrationless as two cylinders could be, and, above all, flexible. Their engines, unlike most cars of the period, could be throttled down to a slow ka-poom, ka-poom, and then by merely opening the throttle wound up to a wild 1000 rpm or so. Most other cars of the day required much diddling with carburetor air and spark controls for any considerable variation in speed. Royce had certainly succeeded in building a better car than his old Decauville. He might even have succeeded in building a better car than any in the world, excepting perhaps the Panhard-Levassor.

The English agent for the Panhard, Charles S. Rolls, heard about the remarkable Royce car. A luncheon was arranged between Rolls and Royce. Rolls then tried out the Royce, was captivated, and soon a new car came to be: Rolls-Royce.

The Hon. Charles Stewart Rolls was an aristocrat, a famous racing driver, an esteemed writer about cars, an aeronaut, and a balloonist. (In 1910 he was killed in a Wright biplane which crashed from an altitude of twenty feet.) He wasn't entirely enamored of two-cylinder cars and soon the new company was building three- and four-cylinder Rolls-Royces. (Only six three-cylinder jobs were built.)

Not only were these cars an immediate commercial success, they did well in competition, too, winning the Tourist Trophy in 1905, on a four-cylinder, light 20 (hp), breaking the record from Monte Carlo to London. Rolls even took a 20 to the United States and won the Silver Trophy race on the Empire City Track in, of all places,

TOP: 1914 *Silver Ghost; body is in vogue of the twenties, when wooden deckwork was all the rage.*
BOTTOM: *A 25/30-hp coupe of the mid-thirties. It was from an earlier 20/25-hp version of this small Rolls-Royce that semisporting 3½-litre Bentley was developed.*

Yonkers. At Ormond Beach, Florida, a 20 also broke the world's five-mile record for cars up to 60 hp against a 70-hp American Mercedes, a Stanley Steamer, a Winton, and a 50-hp Welch (the very machine I now own and which was then owned by L. H. Perlman).

When Rolls returned to London he made some uncomplimentary remarks about American cars which much annoyed E. R. Thomas, builder of the American Thomas Flyer, a crude copy of the French Brasier. Thomas and Perlman both challenged Royce to a race within thirty days, a time limit obviously impossible for Royce to meet. He disdainfully turned down both gentlemen's challenges but suggested they enter the Tourist Trophy. Neither did.

In 1906 Rolls-Royce went off the track, briefly, in an *affaire* with an idiosyncratic vehicle called the Legalimit, which meant that it was to proceed at no more than 20 miles an hour, then the legal speed limit in Britain. It was to be a town carriage as quiet and smokeless as an electric. In fact this gutless wonder was to be so much like an electric that in one model, the Invisible Engine Landaulet, it was to appear as if it had no gasoline engine at all. Its power plant was hidden someplace in the cellar under the living quarters.

To this end a most ingenious engine, a very flat and shallow V8 with full-pressure lubrication, was designed, which was indeed flexible, smokeless, and vibrationless. But the whole project, although it had been announced with much trumpeting, died after only two or three cars were built. Who, even in 1906, would want a car that was *designed* to be a sluggard?

After the debacle of the Legalimit, Royce got back on course. He continued the natural progression from two, to four, to six cylinders, first with the not-too-successful 30 hp and then, as we have seen, with the *sans pareil* Silver Ghost.

The Ghost remained in production until 1926, with modifications, of course, like modern coil ignition in addition to its magneto, aluminum pistons, and, toward the end, front-wheel brakes. In 1919 an American company in Springfield, Massachusetts, was formed to build Ghosts. The early productions were almost exactly like the products of the parent company, but later machines gradually departed more and more from the English designs.

But the Ghost was getting a bit long in the tooth. Other makes were catching up and in some respects even surpassing the Ghost. Hispano-Suiza, Isotta-Fraschini, Bentley, and even some Americans like Packard and Lincoln were breathing hard down Rolls-Royce's neck.

Hoping to uphold its position Rolls-Royce brought out a new model, the New Phantom (the Phantom I).

The great difference between the 40/50 Silver Ghost and the new Phantom was in its 100-hp engine, which now had pushrod-operated overhead valves and a slightly larger capacity: 7668 cc instead of 7428. It still retained the torque-tube drive and the long cantilever rear springs of the Ghost. But to help the driver stop this heavy mass of machinery—often over 6,000 pounds with closed coachwork—a servo brake mechanism, operated by way of a clutch at the side of the gearbox, augmented the muscles of the driver's right leg. This device was an improved version of that used on the Hispano-Suiza, and Rolls paid Hispano a fee for it.

Almost all of the P-I's which were used

in this country were built in the Springfield factory, perhaps because they had left-hand drive. The Massachusetts car differed from the British-built machines in having a three-speed gearbox operated by a centrally located gear lever. The English machines were, of course, fitted with right-hand steering and a right-hand gear lever working in a gate; further, they had the four speeds insisted upon by Britons even though they seldom used more than two of them. The British-built jobs also had magneto ignition for six of the twelve spark plugs, a coil for the rest. The American Royce used two coils, no magneto, and also used American instruments of superlative quality especially made for it.

I have owned two of these Springfield P-I's. One was a beautifully bodied Derby Phaeton by Brewster with only 17,000 miles on its clock, which I bought in 1937 for $275. (Its German owner, a mouth-organ tycoon, was in a sweat during the early Hitler period to get rid of anything with an English taint.) The other was a Riviera town car (also by Brewster), whose tiny passenger compartment made its inmates feel as if they were riding in a luxurious phone booth. Both machines were lovely to look at. Their mechanisms were of expectedly superb intricacy and finish. Yet driving and maintaining them was somewhat less than a joy. Perhaps the heavy torque tubes bouncing at their aft ends, plus the front-braked front axles and their thick-sectioned tires, had something to do with it, but the P-I's certainly did not have the delicacy of control of a good Ghost. They were, however, fairly quick machines for their type; a rather unhappy 80 was possible.

Maintenance always was a problem. Their one-shot lubrication systems, carrying lubri-cating oil down a multiplicity of pipes, were continually out of kilter. Some leaked, some clogged. Oil always seemed to reach the clutch facings of the brake servo. Timing gears rattled ominously. Perhaps it was my fault for not being rich enough to hire a man and a boy to devote themselves to carrying out the endless maintenance instructions in the voluminous instruction book. Nor, as a resident of the United States, was I able to avail myself of Rolls-Royce's offer to send an engineer to my home to adjust things. Further, I could neither send my cars to the factory every fifty thousand miles for "dismantling and inspection" as Rolls-Royce advised, nor go to Rolls-Royce's excellent school which taught paid drivers (or less pecunious owners) the secrets of maintenance. Had I been able to do these things I'm sure my cars would have lasted forever, as Rolls-Royces should.

I had similar problems with a 1935 Continental Phantom II (the P-II succeeded the P-I in 1929), but it was a much improved machine. The torque tube was gone, as were the cantilever springs. The Continental Touring model was a particularly fine version of the standard P-II. It had flatter springs, a higher compression ratio than standard, and a higher rear-axle ratio.

The P-II Continental was fast. Its 160-hp engine enabled it to whip from 0 to 60 in 19½ seconds and exceed 95 mph (I saw 100 on my clock several times), which was better than many a sports car of its day. Its steering was smooth, its roadholding very fine. My car—a late one (187 TA)—had synchromesh on its top three gears and I don't remember ever handling a nicer gearbox. I wish I hadn't sold it, and I wouldn't have if I had been able to afford sending it back to its birthplace for "dismantling and inspection."

The P-II was, in a way, the last of the 40/50's which had descended in a straight line from the 40/50 Silver Ghosts. But in 1923 a smaller machine, built to fit the slightly shrunken purses of the post-Kaiser War period, had nosed its way among its nobler sisters. This was the "baby" Rolls-Royce, the 20 hp. (This business of rating an engine at 20 hp or 40/50 hp is meaningless today. It was an artificial system of ratings based on cylinder diameters and devised by the British for tax purposes.)

This 20 engine developed about 50 hp. It had six cylinders, overhead valves, and a cubic capacity of 3150 cc. In fact, its design foreshadowed the engine of the Phantom I. Enthusiasts of the period sneered at the new baby, not only because of its stodgy performance—its top speed wasn't much over 60— but because it had a centrally located gear lever and only three speeds, a dismal bit of Americanism in British eyes. (It was changed to four speeds in a right-hand gate, a year later.) In spite of this carping the baby was a quite successful machine, fast enough for the stuffy types who bought it. Further it handled very sweetly on the two-lane roads which curled so eccentrically over the map of England. It was, in fact, the precursor of Rolls-Royces and Rolls-built Bentleys almost until the present day. From it stemmed the 20/25, the 25/30, the Wraith, and the prewar Bentley.

The Rolls-built Bentley was based on the 20/25 Rolls-Royce and was in no wise similar to the old groundshakers built by the original Bentley Motors Limited, whose assets Rolls bought up in 1931—including the services of W. O. Bentley, who had no hand in the design of the new car bearing his name. The first of these "silent sports cars,"

which appeared in 1933, had a 3½-litre engine which differed from that in the 20/25 in several ways. It had a new head, twin S.U. carburetors instead of the single Rolls-built breathing device of the 20/25, and a higher compression ratio. Power output was about 110 hp.

Its chassis was entirely different from that of the 20/25. Lower and more in the sporting tradition, it was based on an experimental chassis which had been designed for a new, smaller, 2¾-litre Rolls which had died in birth.

Although no twitchy, nervous, super-sports bomb, the new Bentley fooled the groaners who wept into their pints of bitter about the rape of the old name. I joined them in their weeping, but we were only partly right. True, the Bentley was now a bit too civilized for the wind-in-the-face, thunder-in-the-ears boys, but it was a most delectably smooth, fast means of sporting transport. This was especially so after 1936, when its engine size was increased to 4¼ litres. A 4¼ Bentley was no slouch in its day—0 to 60 in 15 seconds, 95 or better. The only thing that put me off somewhat, at least in the heavy-bodied Thrupp and Maberly convertible I owned, was its tendency to lose its road grip aft if I took a corner too quickly.

The Rolls-Bentley did surprisingly well in racing, too—a role for which it had certainly not been built. E. R. Hall, for example, modified several cars with the help of Rolls-Royce, although he had to enter them privately since the factory wouldn't dream of going racing. He made the fastest time in three Tourist Trophy races, but never placed better than second due to the handicapping. In a 3½ litre in 1935 he averaged 80.36 mph for 478 miles, faster than the 3.3-

1934 P-III Rolls-Royce had V-12 engine, independent front suspension. This was the first Rolls-Royce in which Henry Royce had no hand. Note black Rolls-Royce insignia which appeared after Royce's death in 1933.

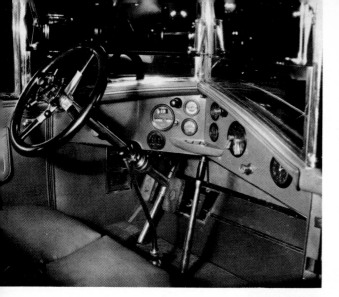

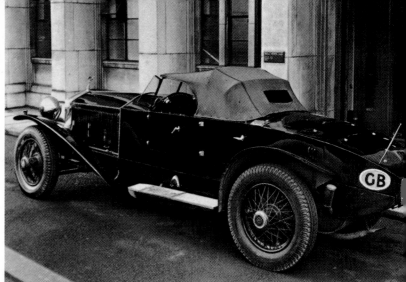

ABOVE LEFT: *Driver's compartment of an American-built Springfield P-I. This car has Locke body with typical V-shaped instrument panel.*

ABOVE RIGHT: *Phantom I 16 EX, one of three cars built in 1928 to test innovations in forthcoming Phantom II.*

RIGHT: *A 4½-litre Bentley of the late thirties. Rolls-built Bentley, which first appeared in 1933 as a 3½-litre car, has nothing in common with Bentley-built cars, except their radiator shell.*

BELOW: *Current Silver Shadow Rolls-Royce retains more or less traditional radiator shape on body of uninspired design.*

litre Bugatti driven by Lord Howe. In 1936 in a 4¼, he put up the best time ever for the T.T., but still couldn't win.

In 1939 George Eyston, the famed land speed-record driver, put 114.7 miles on the clock in one hour at Brooklands Track. This was done with a specially modified Mark V Bentley built for Walter Sleator. The Mark V had independent front suspension. Fewer than twenty were built before Hitler put a stop to production. A Corniche model based on Sleator's special Mark V was next on Rolls' list, but while the prototype sat on the dock at Dieppe, dressed in a new French-built body by Van Vooren, Goering's Stukas blew it to bits.

In 1933 Henry Royce died and the Rolls-Royce badge changed from red to black. He had for many years been gravely ill and had been away from the factory. In his homes in the south of France and in Sussex, however, he had been closely involved with every bit of the design of his cars.

The first car in which Henry Royce had no hand was the Rolls-Royce P-III, which appeared in 1936 and was built until war broke out in 1939. This new car has been called a masterpiece of complication. Although complication is no sin if you never have to delve into it, the P-III — V-12 engined and with General Motors licensed independent front suspension — ofttimes did require a modicum of delving, mostly due to the hydraulically controlled valve tappets. Nowadays, with our detergent oils, these tappets would most likely give no trouble. But the oils of the thirties tended to sludge in the passages leading to the tappets, seizing them solid and thus raising hob with the cams. And "dismantling and inspecting" a P-III engine requires the income of a Gulbenkian. Such sludging would not, of course,

happen to people who went through the oiling and filter-cleaning rituals laid down in the R-R manual. But few did. And most P-III's today have been converted to solid tappets.

Aside from this annoying engine malaise, the P-III was without a doubt one of the very greatest luxury cars of all time. Fast — although perhaps not quite as fast as a good P-II Continental — superbly sprung, and a delight to drive, I'd as soon have one as any super-luxury car of today.

During the second German war, as it had during the first, Rolls-Royce built the engines for the British aircraft which helped smash the Boche bombing squadrons. When the war ended, R-R went back to building superb motorcars. But not entirely. Now Rolls' chief concern is in building big engines for the jet age; the car business is a secondary source of income. But while the world has changed and honest craftsmanship has all but disappeared, a Rolls-Royce is still one of man's great artifacts.

True, Rolls no longer makes every bit of its cars in its own shops. Carburetors, ignition systems, cylinder castings, and other parts are bought from outsiders. But a Rolls is still a Rolls, tested and examined and retested and babied and polished like no other car. The MK VI Bentley, the Silver Wraith, the Silver Dawns and Clouds, and the Bentleys (which are now exactly like Rolls-Royces except for their easier-to-make radiator shells) are worth more when they reach old age than any other car on earth.

Will the new Silver Shadow — with its disc brakes, self-leveling mechanism, and other super-modern appurtenances — uphold the great name? I'm sure it will. Especially if they get rid of that damned imitation Nash Rambler body.

BENTLEY

EU 919

BENTLEY

For years and years the British were the poor relations of motor racing. Although they built nice sports cars, they only very rarely won an international sports-car race. And no one dreamed that the bumbling English would ever get any place at all in Grand Prix racing.

I had long thought that this was why the British and their anglophile adherents deified the old "big green Bentleys" of Le Mans. And why, along with this deification, they also magnified the importance of the *vingt-quatre heures du Mans* out of all proportion. After all, the Bentleys *must* have won an *important* race.

But times have changed. The British are the near masters of motor racing. It is no longer necessary to look back nostalgically at ancient victories, or at the cars which won them. But the Bentley cult continues. I was at least partly wrong; people (and include me, please) love those old Bentleys for other reasons beside the fact that they won in the days when other British machines seemed to make a habit of losing. Why?

The Bentleys from first to last—a mere twelve years—were honestly, beautifully constructed motorcars built by an honest man, Walter Owen Bentley, who had the same feel for carved and cast metal that Henry Royce had. For like Royce, he had served the grueling, five-year apprenticeship in the locomotive shops of the Great Northern Railway. Further, although built to keep on running without fault or breakage, Bentleys were meant to move rapidly, to steer positively, to look wonderful. And after forty years those old Bentleys still act and look as they were designed to.

I saw my first Bentley—a 1927 Red Label 3-litre Speed Model—in 1930. It was the proudest possession of a friend, and I covered many happy miles in it. To our present-day eyes the 3-litre Bentley looks high and stumpy, but compared to the Detroit-built machinery of that time it was racily low-slung. And, of course, its exciting performance made most American cars seem stodgy and boring. But it wasn't only performance which made us love that Bentley so. Everything about it was different and intriguing— its instrument panel full of high-quality round gauges; its accurate finish, not only of the engine, but also of things like brake and gear-shift levers.

This 3-litre Red Label was capable of close to 90 mph; I think 87 was the highest speed I ever saw on the speedometer. There was also a special Green Label short-chassis 100-MPH Model. But the short chassis was likely to go slightly sideways if you got too exuberant on a wet road. The 1927 Speed Model developed almost 90 hp from its long stroke (80 x 149 mm) engine. It had a nondetachable head, four valves per cylinder, dual magneto ignition, a single-overhead camshaft, and twin S.U. carburetors. The camshaft was driven from a vertical shaft at the front of the engine. The chassis was quite conventional, with half-elliptic springs all around, four-wheel brakes, and a close-ratio four-speed gearbox that took a bit of knowing.

Walter O. Bentley had built his first car in time for the 1919 show at Olympia in London. Like the 37.2 Hispano-Suiza to which it bore a remarkable resemblance (as pointed out by my good friend Alec Ulmann, the knowledgeable enthusiast who puts on the twelve-hour races at Sebring), its engine owed much to the advances in design resulting from the development of World War I's aircraft engines. Also, since W. O. Bentley wanted to build a high-performance sporting

Imposing bluff-bowed 4½-litre "blower" Bentley had square yards of frontal area to push through the air. Only fifty of these 105-mph machines were built.

The 4½-litre "blower" Bentley again. It seems almost inconceivable today that such truck-like vehicles ran, and often won, at Le Mans. This supercharged type, however, never won any races. LEFT: Supercharger sat in vulnerable position forward of radiator. Wire shield protects carburetors. ABOVE: Dash has more dials than WWI Handley Page bomber.

car, he took a hard look at the racing engines used by Mercedes and Peugeot just before war broke out.

Bentley himself had learned much about high-performance engines during the war. He had been the designer of the successful B.R.1 and B.R.2 (B.R. for Bentley Rotary) engines which had powered British fighter aircraft. Bentley, too, had been the first man to use aluminum pistons in the engines of the French D.F.P. (Doriet, Flandrin et Parent; he had the English concession for this marque, which he raced quite successfully before the war). And it was Bentley who had convinced the British military of the advantages of the aluminum pistons which soon became standardized in the aero engines of the Allies.

Almost immediately, the Bentley became the "in" car of the gilded young Britons of Mayfair's *beau monde,* despite a thumping price of one thousand guineas in chassis form. And an even more "in" group, "The Bentley Boys," devoted themselves to racing the thunderous green cars.

Oddly, one of the first big races in which a 3-litre Bentley was entered was the Indianapolis "500." They must have been out of their minds. But the Bentley did better than you might expect—at least it finished. No one seems to know exactly where. Some say thirteenth, others fifteenth or twentieth.

But as we've noted, it was at Le Mans that the Bentleys created their mystique. They won five times—in 1924, 1927, 1928, 1929, and 1930. Twice they took both first and second, and in 1929 the four Bentleys entered took the first four places.

They were not all 3-litre machines, of course. Later brawnier, bigger machines— the 4½ litre, the blown 4½, and the 6½ litre (Big Six)—raced, too. Some models never raced, notably that lovely giant the 8 litre.

The 3-litre Bentley was the most popular of all—1,639 were sold during the six years of its production and accounted for over half of the 3,061 Bentleys ever built (not including the Rolls-built Bentleys).

In 1926 the Bix Six (with the identical 100 x 140 mm bore and stroke of the 37.2 Hispano-Suiza) went into production. This engine also had an overhead camshaft, but instead of gear drive the camshaft was driven by three thin connecting rods attached to eccentrics on the crankshaft and camshaft. Wonderfully quiet—W. O. Bentley disliked mechanical noise—they looked like something stolen off the flank of one of the Atlantic-class locomotives Bentley fired when he was an apprentice. Later, in 1929, there was a more sporting version of this machine called the Speed Six. At Le Mans these Speed Sixes often bettered 100 mph.

The birth of the 6½-litre Bentley was due to a strange coincidence. The Bentley Factory was experimenting with the prototype of a 4¼-litre six. To this end they fitted the chassis with an extraordinarily ugly sedan body and disguised its front end with an angular radiator shell of particularly nauseating appearance. This dismal-looking equipage was yclept The Sun, and was so registered. Then Bentley and three confreres hied themselves off to the straight roads of France for a spot of testing and also to watch the 1924 French Grand Prix. At the same time they took the opportunity to try out the then-new Dunlop balloon tires, which although comfortably soft, blew out with deadly frequency. Even though they had wired London for more tires, they were down to their last set as they sped homeward. They were rapidly approaching a Y junction as another strange-looking and unrecognizable car raced for the junction on the other leg. Neither of them gave way and both cars flew into the stem of the Y side by side. Both parties immediately saw through the camouflage. The other car was the new Phantom I Rolls-Royce, also on test. Both drivers stamped on their accelerators and roared along side by side, filling the narrow tree-lined *route nationale*, neither managing to best the other, kilometer after kilometer, up and down hill. They'd very likely have run right on into the English Channel had not the cap of one of the Rolls-Royce's passengers blown off. The Rolls stopped to retrieve it and the Bentley went on. The Rolls' speed worried the Bentley people and to ensure their superiority, since they were certain their speed would also spur Rolls-Royce to increase the power of the P-I, the new Bentley's cubic capacity was increased from 4¼ to 6½ litres.

Bentley fanciers seem to like the 4½-litre model above all the others. This four-cylinder machine, which first came out in 1927, had many engine parts interchangeable with the 6½ litre since its cylinder dimensions were the same. The camshaft is driven, however, like that on the 3-litre engines, by means of a vertical shaft. With 110 horsepower the 4½ was not as much faster than the late 3-litre jobs as you might think. In standard trim, 92 mph was just about its maximum, mostly because it was considerably beefier and heavier. But 4½'s had a wonderful racing career, especially at Le Mans, which race they first won in 1928 with Woolf Barnato and Bernard Rubin covering 1,658.6 miles at an average of 69.11 mph. In the same race Sir Henry (Tim) Birkin put up the fastest lap at 79.5 mph.

Birkin, in 1930, ran his own team of supercharged Bentleys under the patronage of the very rich, the Honorable Dorothy Paget and in competition with the factory team. In a way it was Birkin's use of the supercharger which, at least partly, caused the old Bentley company finally to go under. W. O. Bentley hated superchargers. In his autobiography he said, "to supercharge a Bentley engine was to pervert its design and corrupt its performance.... When people ask me why Bentleys went bust I usually give three reasons: the slump, the 4-litre car, and the 'blower' 4½'s; in proportions of about 70, 20 and 10% respectively." (The 4 litre was a stodgy pushrod-engined disaster which the company directors insisted on building when things looked black toward the end in 1931.)

But in 1930, by which time W. O. Bentley had lost control of his company and was unable to prevent it, fifty "blower" 4½'s were built in order to meet the Le Mans regulations. A "blower" Bentley looks wonderful with that lovely complicated supercharger, plus its S.U. carburetors out in front of the radiator. In spite of its 105-mph speed, however, no blown 4½ ever won a race.

Like many builders of superfine motor-cars, Bentley Motors often skated on the edge of insolvency. As early as 1926, a transfusion of many gold guineas was necessary in order to keep the company alive. W. O. Bentley turned to Barnato, one of the "Bentley Boys," for help.

"Babe" Barnato was the son of the fabulous Barney Barnato who, with Cecil Rhodes, owned the Kimberly diamond mines in South Africa. When Barney Barnato disappeared overboard while sailing home from Africa with two-year-old Woolf, the tot became very wealthy indeed. He grew up to be the best of the Bentley drivers as well, according

ABOVE: *In 1921 a 3-litre Bentley
ran in the Indianapolis "500" with little success.* LEFT:
*8-litre Bentley engine. Normally, engine had
two carburetors; this is a three-carburetor conversion.*

ABOVE RIGHT: *1927 3-litre Bentley.
This was most popular type of all the Bentleys:
1,639 were sold in six years. They
were capable of little over 80 mph, but their
roadholding and handling were far
superior to most cars of mid-twenties. One above has
typical Vanden Plas fabric coachwork.*

RIGHT: *Similar car with unusual
two-seater boat-tailed body.*
FAR RIGHT: *An 8-litre Bentley with
Weymann fabric coachwork.*

ABOVE: *A 1930 Speed Six Bentley. Bentley chassis were meticulously constructed works of art, but some of the ugliest coachwork of all time was often erected on them. This coupe has what we call a rumble seat. British called it a "dickey."*

RIGHT: *Engine of a 3-litre Bentley. Note that twin S.U. carburetors are early "slopers." Drive for overhead camshaft is in tube at right of engine.*

BELOW RIGHT: *Engine of 4½-litre "blower" Bentley. The twin protuberances are supercharger blow-off valves.*

OPPOSITE: *British enthusiasts pinned epithet "the Bentley Boys" on small, select group of men who raced Bentleys to victory at Le Mans. Among them were Sir Henry Birkin, J. D. Benjafield, S. C. H. Davis, S. C. Clement, Bernard Rubin, Jack Dunfee, Glen Kidston, and, of course, Woolf Barnato. In picture taken at Le Mans, W. O. Bentley (wearing business suit) is fourth man from the right.*

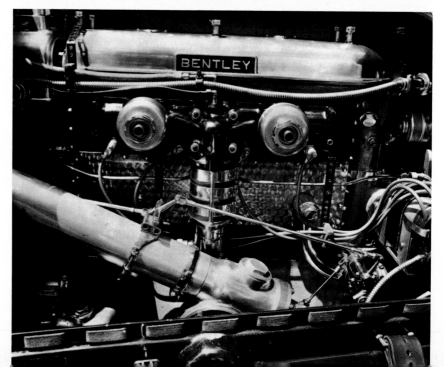

104

to Bentley himself. Barnato's millions kept Bentley Motors afloat for the next five years. It cost him £90,000, but he seems to have got his money's worth. After all, he did become chairman of Bentley Motors and, naturally, could drive on the team anytime he felt the urge.

In 1930 a different kind of Bentley appeared. This fabulous carriage was designed not as a sporting vehicle (the racing successes and the super-sports image of earlier models had frightened off some possible buyers), but as a rapid and luxurious equipage for the same rich types who might go for Rolls-Royces. This was the awesome 8-litre Bentley. Most of these bore formidably heavy limousine coachwork, but a few had open sporting bodies on a special short chassis — 144 inches compared to the standard 156 inches! At one time, when a friend of mine owned such a machine, I did a fair amount of driving in it. Surprisingly, it handled quite as easily as 4½- and 3-litre Bentleys I've driven, although it turned in a circle only slightly smaller than that required by the old *Mauretania*. And it was fast! The engine was almost exactly like that in the Speed Six, complete with eccentric drive for the camshaft, but its extra cubic capacity gave it a more zestful performance.

I never drove it at much more than 100 or so but my friend claims to have seen 110 on the speedometer. He sold it a few years ago for some $15,000.

Suitably lightened and tuned (often by Bentley-expert Mackenzie), 8 litres are often much faster. Forrest Lycett's famous example was timed, in 1956, at 141.7 mph for the flying kilometer. Only one hundred 8-litre machines were built. After all, $9,000 was a lot of money for a chassis in 1931.

That was the last year for the big green Bentleys. The depression was beginning to bite. Barnato decided against pouring any more pounds away. Bentley went into receivership and for a while there was a glimmer of hope. Napier's, long famous as car builders until 1925, negotiated to buy up the company and even had W. O. Bentley design a new car, the Napier-Bentley, a slimmer and sleeker 6¼-litre version of the 8 litre.

When, in court at the receiver's sale, Napier's put in their bid for the company, it was thought to be a mere formality. No other bids were expected.

But another bidder, the British Central Equitable Trust, showed up, offered a very slightly higher price, and got the company.

Who was B. C. E. T. representing?

Rolls-Royce, of course.

DUESENBERG

DUESENBERG I really don't believe that we could build and sell a Model J Duesenberg here in the United States today. I mean just an honest-to-god duplicate, without incorporating anything we've learned about braking and suspension, which are the only real improvements in motorcars in the last thirty years or so.

I suppose you could, if you paid enough, entice some machinists away from whittling the multifarious moon vehicles that now seem so important. These mechanical gentlemen might be able to duplicate a Duesenberg's engine and chassis, and perhaps even its instruments, but where in the U.S.A. would you be able to construct those lovely, toughly built bodies Duesenbergs wore? The answer is no place. The great custom auto body designers and builders who descended from the old carriage builders are gone for good. Their traditions have disappeared, along with their apprentice systems which taught each new generation the craft of the past.

Custom body builders are just about gone elsewhere in the world, too—except to a limited extent in Italy. Perhaps, then, we could duplicate a Duesenberg engine and chassis and bolt an Italian body on it. What would it cost? I don't think it could be done for less than $100,000 per car. At which price you'd sell no cars.

These speculations may serve to remind us of what we've lost. For back in 1928 this country had the technical ability to produce one of the very great cars of all time. And you could buy one for what now seems a low price: $14,000. Today if you could buy one in fair shape at twice that price you'd be lucky.

In 1928, however, a $14,000 Duesenberg was strictly for millionaires; with extra-fancy bodywork a Duesenberg might cost up to $25,000. But they certainly got their money's worth, for the Duesenberg was not only as prestigious and vast as a Rolls-Royce or an Isotta-Fraschini, it also gave its lucky owner the speed and power and excitement of a near-racing machine—a combination almost unimaginable back in 1928, when 100 hp and 90 mph were considered exceptional.

The J Duesenberg offered 265 hp and 116 mph; 90 mph in second gear! The only comparable car of its day was the monstrous 13-litre Bugatti Royale, which developed 300 hp from an engine twice the Duesenberg's size and was said to be capable of 125 mph. But, in chassis form, sans body, the Royale cost $30,000.

The straight-eight Duesenberg engine had a capacity of almost 7 litres. Twin chain-driven, overhead camshafts operated four valves per cylinder. The engine's connecting rods and pistons were of aluminum, its beautifully machined crankshaft was of chrome-nickel steel and had five hefty main bearings $2\frac{3}{4}$ inches in diameter. An unusual feature of this crankshaft was the means employed to damp out vibration. Cartridges ninety-four per cent full of mercury were bolted to the crank cheek between cylinders No. 1 and No. 2. The inertia of the mercury sloshing around in the cartridges absorbed the torsional vibrations of the long shaft. The Duesenberg engine developed its peak power at frighteningly high revs for its long stroke ($4\frac{3}{4}$ inches) and heavy reciprocating parts, but Fred Duesenberg, its designer, and the Lycoming factory where the engines were built knew what they were about, for hundreds of Duesenberg engines are still running, although many of them do require expensive nursing care. A friend of mine recently spent more than $3,000 simply

108

PRECEDING PAGES: 1935 J *Duesenberg roadster.*
It took sheer arrogance to use almost three tons of
machinery and 265 horsepower to transport
two persons to golf course. This car also had rumble seat
for servant and golf-bag compartment.

*Duesenberg built racing machines as early as
1913. In 1914 a Duesenberg driven by Eddie Rickenbacker
took tenth place in the Indianapolis "500."
Rickenbacker is man at left walking toward cars.*

to have an engine overhauled.

The Duesenberg had a three-speed gearbox, a two-plate clutch, torque-tube drive, a ladder-type chassis frame, semielliptic springing. All of this sounds very ordinary, but each bit was built, Duesenberg-style, of the very best materials. The chassis frame, for example, was 8½ inches deep with six cross members. The semifloating rear axles, bored out to save weight, were no less than 2 3/16 inches in diameter.

When you climb into the driving compartment of a Duesenberg, it seems high, narrow, and strangely old-fashioned. The long, centrally positioned gear lever and the handbrake look cheap and overly simple. Some-

how the driving compartment is unsatisfying, until you start to examine that dashboard.

The instrument panel of a Duesenberg must have cost almost as much to build as its engine. It had an altimeter-barometer, a tachometer, a stopwatch-chronometer, a brake pressure gauge, plus all the usual instruments. But Duesenberg dashboards had something more to tickle their drivers: four idiot lights with a high I.Q. One light went on every 1,500 miles to warn the driver to put water in the battery. Another glowed at each 750-mile oil-change interval. Two others were hooked up to the automatic chassis lubricator. If oil was proceeding correctly to the multifarious places that re-

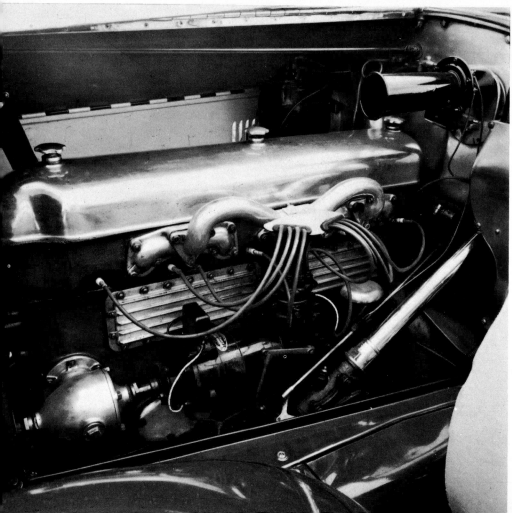

ABOVE: 1933 SJ Duesenberg
supercharged speedster, with
outside exhaust pipe. The
SJ's blower was of centrifugal
type and had little
effect at low engine speeds.
This body was
designed by Gordon Buehrig;
coffin-nosed 810 Cord
also was Buehrig design.
Duesenberg brothers'
first car was Model A, built
from 1920 until E. L. Cord
took over in 1926.

LEFT: Uncluttered,
well-designed straight-eight
engine that powered car.

RIGHT: 1925 Duesenberg model
has rather dull-looking
body that helped keep sales down.

ABOVE CENTER: *If you were close enough to read "stop" on J's and SJ's distinctive rear light, it was too late to stop.* ABOVE: *J's well-filled instrument panel.*

TOP: *Duesenbergs took first place at Indianapolis in 1924, 1925, and 1927. This is Bill Spence in his 1929 Duesenberg Special.*
ABOVE: *SJ supercharged Brunn-bodied Torpedo Phaeton. Car had disappearing top.*

quired a shot of lubricant—say, the right front steering knuckle or the clutch throw-out bearing—a red light flashed contentedly. If the oil reservoir had run dry, a green light balefully accused you.

A Duesenberg takes a bit of getting used to. It doesn't feel like a fast car; it really isn't terribly quick by modern standards. In fact, it feels almost sluggish and heavy unless you look at the speedometer. And you'd better watch that speedometer, especially on a twisting road. For although a Duesenberg's roadholding was excellent by American standards of thirty-five years ago, it's not exactly the car to stick close behind a Lotus on a corner, or even a modern Chevrolet, for that matter.

Perhaps the SJ supercharged Duesenbergs, especially the short-chassis (142½-inch wheelbase) roadsters, could do better. I don't know. I've never driven one. But purportedly one of these hotter types would go from 0 to 100 in 17 seconds!

These Duesenbergs came out in 1932 and had centrifugal blowers which at full bore spun at some 24,000 rpm! A centrifugal blower isn't much at low engine speeds, but the SJ engine was said to develop some 320 hp when you dared put your foot down. One hundred and four mph was claimed in second gear, 130 mph in high.

Duesenberg was primarily a chassis builder. Some of their most beautiful bodies were designed in their own shop by that American genius, Gordon Buehrig, who designed the 810 Cord, and many were built by La Grande, which was Duesenberg owned. But others were built by the great American *carossiers* which were still afloat in those depression years: Murphy, Locke, Le Baron, Judkins, and others. A fair number of very lovely bodies also were built for decaying royalty and business bigwigs by outfits in Europe like Figoni-Falaschi, Franay, and Hibbard and Darrin.

It's surprising how many people imagine that the Duesenberg (made in Indianapolis) was a German car. The Duesenberg brothers, Fred and August, were born in Germany, but arrived here as children. Fred Duesenberg was the self-taught engineering genius of the pair and had, as early as 1903, built a racing car. By 1921 a Duesenberg driven by Jimmy Murphy became the first and only American car to win the French Grand Prix. In 1924, 1925, and 1927 Duesenbergs won the Indianapolis "500."

The Duesenberg brothers' first passenger car, their Model A, which came out in 1920, had many features based on their racing experience. It was light, with an uncommonly large amount of aluminum in its structure, had four-wheel hydraulic brakes (a Duesenberg innovation) and a 90-hp straight-eight engine. Although of first-class construction and with better road manners than almost any car of its day, the Model A was rather prosaic looking for a $6,500 car and didn't sell well. In 1926, Erret Lobban Cord, an ex-car salesman who had made it big with the sharp-looking but cheap Auburn, acquired control of Duesenberg.

So in 1928, with Auburn money behind it and the Herbert Hoover years of "two chickens in every pot and two cars in every garage" ahead of it, the J Duesenberg was born. By 1937, when production ended, some five hundred had been built. Fred Duesenberg died in 1932, after an accident in one of his cars. He didn't live to see the day when a Duesenberg, full of years and many, many miles, would be cherished as a great American artifact and would be worth twice its original cost.

113

Frazer Nash

PRECEDING PAGES: 1934 *Blackburne-engined*
Frazer Nash. Driver was as far outdoors as he could
get and still not be aboard a motorcycle.
Even if he were so effete as to put up top in a
rainstorm, his right arm still got wet.

Two chain-gangsters in hill-climbing
competition. TOP: *Sporting "Nash" (non-standard*
fenders) at Prescott, Bugatti owners' club
hill. ABOVE: *A.F.P. Fane in single-seater at*
Shelsley Walsh. Note dual rear wheels.

Frazer Nash Of all the many vintage sports cars I've never owned, the one I yearn for is the chain-drive Frazer Nash. It was a frantic, spiky, spidery, nervous, quick machine, a sort of high-strung motorcycle with four wheels. I do believe that if you were to bolt a pair of motorcycles together and then sit down between them, controlling their front wheels with a steering wheel, you'd get a sensation not unlike that of driving a Frazer Nash.

Writing about other, more mundane motorcars, you can set down a chronicle of models and model changes in some sort of sensible progression. But not with Frazer Nashes. For there were so many models: Boulogne, Colmore, Exeter, Fast Tourer, T. T. Replica, Falcon, Le Mans Replica, Interceptor, Ulster, etc., etc., and so many different engines—Anzani, Meadows, Gough, Blackburne, four and six cylinder, supercharged and unsupercharged—that the mind boggles at sorting them out. Further, the Aldington Brothers would screw together almost any combination of engine, chassis, and body you wanted.

Still, a Frazer Nash was uniquely a Frazer Nash, unlike any other car because of a multiple-chain drive which incorporated its means of changing gear. Furthermore, a Frazer Nash had no differential gear or much in the way of springing. Four quarter-elliptics helped keep the car from being shaken to pieces on rough roads; obviously, the comfort of its driver and passenger was of secondary importance to its builders. Agility was a strong point, but the driver had to keep his wits about him, for the steering of many Frazer Nashes required no more than seven-eighths of a turn from lock to lock.

Certainly many of these characteristics were common to other sports cars of the twenties and thirties, but the Frazer Nash had something they didn't have—its wondrous and fearsome chain drive.

Roughly, here's how chain drive worked. From the clutch behind the engine a short drive shaft led to a pair of bevel gears inside a cylindrical casing. From the sides of this casing protruded a pair of shafts carrying a series of four sprockets and dog clutches. At the rear was another shaft joining the rear wheels, and another set of four sprockets. Each sprocket on the front shaft drove a corresponding sprocket on the rear shaft by means of a roller chain. The four sprockets on the rear shaft varied in size and thus gave four gear ratios. To select any gear —by means of the gear lever and a trick linkage—you merely had to slide one of the dog clutches into mesh with the side of one of the sprockets on the front shaft, locking it to the shaft. You were then in the gear you wanted to be in. The rest of the sprockets and chains then turned freely. This sounds formidable, but it was really very simple. Gear changes could be made easily and with lightning speed. Furthermore, if you didn't like the gear ratios your car came with, or if you wanted special ratios for competition, installing new sprockets on the rear shaft was a cinch. Reverse had a small countershaft of its own.

Most Frazer Nashes had a wonderful look, too. The radiator was set 'way, 'way back of the front axle, which was gripped by the very ends of the quarter-elliptic front springs. The front semicycle-type fenders had a slight sweep aft but their inner sides did not meet the chassis. The driver could actually see his right front brake drum. Skinny outside exhaust pipes curved outward from a strapped-down hood. The narrow, fabric-covered body had a clean sparseness about it and

there was no attempt to hide the chassis frame; brake-rods, for example, were nakedly exposed. Its rounded behind sat partly over a big gas tank with a huge filler sticking out of its middle.

Most Frazer Nashes look as if they might have another pair of seats under their tonneau covers. But they don't. That's where all the chains and sprockets live. There were, however, a few early cars with minimal rear seating.

The fly-off hand brake and gear lever are outside, and even if you're sybaritic enough to erect the top when it rains (which most

chain-gangsters don't), you'll end up with a cold and wet right arm. Unless, of course, you own a bit of British wearing apparel called a "dri-sleeve," which was, in the thirties, advertised for just such a contingency.

On the road, a Frazer Nash is a pretty twitchy mechanism. On corners in the wet, the rear wheels always slide (remember, you have no differential). When it's dry, you make them slide if you want to get around rapidly. But you can straighten up fast with that seven-eighths-of-a-turn steering. A late Frazer Nash with, say, a 1½-litre Blackburne engine like that installed in the 1934 model

TOP LEFT: *More comprehensive view of Blackburne-engined*
Frazer Nash. TOP: *Chains and sprockets of unique transmission.*
Shifting is lightning quick. ABOVE LEFT: *No part of*
running gear is left to the imagination. ABOVE RIGHT: *Twin-camshaft*
1667-cc Blackburne engine developed about 75 hp.

pictured, would approach 90 mph and go from 0 to 60 in under 14 seconds. Cars with more puissant power plants would naturally go faster, but, except for competition jobs, there were very few of them.

The Frazer Nash was not only a delight to handle and an outstandingly safe car because it went exactly where it was pointed, it was also a simple car on which a man could do his own work. Further, a Frazer Nash was comparatively cheap to buy. The cheapest Frazer Nash in the early thirties, with a four-cylinder L-head Meadows engine and three speeds, could be bought for £325, about $1,600. Even a supercharged, overhead-valve-engined Boulogne with four speeds cost only £500, about $2,500. It's hard at this date to understand why more of them weren't snapped up when you compare it with the MG Midget, which wasn't in the same league and at that time cost over $1,000.

The Frazer Nash was the direct descendant of the G.N., a sporting cycle car which had two cylinders and a chain drive not too unlike its offspring. Although the primitive G.N. had been successful in competition and was much loved by a small coterie of "in" types, the day of the cycle car had waned. Captain Archie Frazer-Nash (note the hyphen) and H. R. Godfrey who were running G. N. Motors, Limited, left the company in 1922, not long before it foundered.

Archie Frazer-Nash formed a new company and in 1924 the first Frazer Nash (no hyphen) appeared. The early cars—three were built in 1925—had French-built Ruby or British Plus-Power engines. By 1925 the 1½-litre, 40-hp Anzani engine was "standard," and in that year forty cars were built. In 1926, Frazer Nash's biggest year, forty-four Anzani-engined cars left the works. Later on, the 50-hp four ED overhead-valve Meadows engine became "standard," and in 1933, twenty-seven cars had Meadows engines, nine had twin-overhead-camshaft, 1½-litre, 75-hp Blackburne engines. All together, from 1924 until the very last chain-drive Frazer Nash was assembled to special order in 1938, only about three hundred and fifty cars were built.

In 1928, Captain Frazer-Nash left the company and later on designed the famous "more-power-to-your-elbow" aircraft gun turret, which did much useful work against the Germans. The company then came under the control of H. J. and W. H. Aldington.

The Frazer Nash had been successful in competition under Archie Frazer-Nash, and continued so under the Aldington regime. A. F. P. Fane in a Frazer Nash blown single-seater at Brooklands Track took the Mountain Class F record at 78.30 mph in 1935. In 1936 Fane lapped Brooklands at 121.77 mph. In 1937 Fane took the Shelsley-Walsh hill-climb record in 38.77 seconds. The following year Raymond Mays in an E.R.A. took the record back; he was a hundredth of a second faster. And in 1932, 1933, and 1934 a gaggle of Frazer Nashes did themselves proud in that toughest of rallies, the Alpine trial, winning four *coupes des glaciers*.

But, as early as 1933, the viper that finally was to kill the chain-drive Nash was already about to sting. In that year the Aldingtons bought the British rights to the German B.M.W. Soon the Frazer Nash-B.M.W. became the company's chief concern. In 1936 only sixteen chain-drive cars were sold, in 1937 two, in 1938 and 1939 only one each year.

The postwar Frazer Nash used a modernized version of the B.M.W. engine built by the Bristol Aeroplane Company Limited in England. No chains, though.

Dedicated types in Frazer Nash car club were so annoyed at this 1950-ish chainless Frazer Nash, with British version of prewar B.M.W. engine, that they pulled out and formed their own club. Car on right is 2-litre Le Mans Replica capable of 120 mph and 0 to 50 mph in under 10 seconds.

CORD

CORD It must have been in 1937, in late May, because we were on our way to Indianapolis for the "500." We were in a Plymouth, of all things, and going about as fast as it would move over the flat roads west of the Alleghenies—say, 80 or so. A Cord came up behind us, pulled out, passed, and disappeared ahead. Its manner of going was smooth, silent, surprisingly quick, and it looked wonderful as it moved off ahead of us doing pretty close to 100.

My brother, a friend of his, and I maintained, as I remember, a respectful silence. It had been our habit to scorn Cords. At that time we thought that foreign machines, Bentleys and Alfas and such, were the only motorcars worth bothering with. We were particularly disdainful of the Cord for several reasons. First, it was kin to the cheap and vulgar Auburn. (It was also related to the Duesenberg, but that wasn't a mark against it.) Further, we felt it was over-styled, too "designy," too Hollywood. But, in my own case, what annoyed me most about the Cord was the view under its coffin-shaped hood. If ever there was a rat's nest of pipes and wiring and cast iron in front of a cheap tin firewall, the Cord's engine compartment was it. I had been spoiled by the austere beauty of the views under the hoods of cars like Hispanos or Bugattis.

Not long after that rear-view incident on the way to Indianapolis, I got a chance to drive a supercharged 812 Model Cord. Messy engine compartment or not, it was a real automobile.

Its handling was away ahead of anything Detroit put out thirty years ago. It was no Alfa, but it certainly was no Buick, either. It didn't roll or wallow, its independent front suspension being just stiff enough. On a corner, you knew you were handling a front-drive machine and didn't take your foot off in mid-passage. It was rather more sensitive in this way than a modern Toronado, for example.

The gear shift, unfortunately, was terrible. The gearbox was way out forward, ahead of the V-8 Lycoming engine, and rather than use a long manual linkage the gears were shifted by a Bendix vacuum cylinder lying on top of the box. To shift you worked a miniature lever in a gate. This activated electrical switch gear which, by means of relays, worked the vacuum cylinder when you took your foot off the gas and declutched. The effect was gear pre-selection, since you could choose a gear but not change into it unless you worked the clutch. But the whole operation was abysmally slow and annoying.

The blown 812 Cord nevertheless was fast for its day: 110 mph was possible and 0 to 60 in under 14 seconds. And the Cord felt stable even at its maximum.

The 812 Cord (and the unblown 810) had other nice features: a flat floor aft was one; a near-noiseless body due to one of the first successful attempts at unit construction was another. But it was its unusually well-designed and really beautiful instrument panel that impressed people—and rightly so. In a day when most instrument boards tried to look like cheap radio sets, with instruments of every tortured shape except honest circles, the Cord's airplane-like panel of engine-turned metal with a rev counter, a speedometer, and oil, water, and electrical gauges looked great. It still looks great.

Most people loved the Cord 810 and 812 bodies (the centrifugally blown 812 had chromed outside exhaust pipes), and many present-day Cord lovers still think it a great design. But the body had a serious fault—poor visibility. Its windshield was just too

125

PRECEDING PAGES: *1937 Cord 812. The 812 was the supercharged version of the front-drive Model 810. Its completely disappearing top and low, svelte lines were sensational in the mid-thirties. Blown horsepower was about 190.*

TOP LEFT: *Supercharged 812 Cord sedan. Its windshield is too shallow for good visibility.* FAR LEFT: *Chromed outside exhaust pipes were symbols of supercharged model.* LEFT: *Retractable headlights were hot stuff in the thirties.*

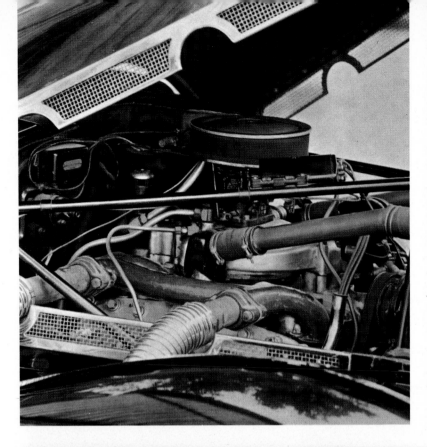

TOP LEFT: *Cord 812's engine was
a monkey jungle of pipes and wiring.* TOP, RIGHT: *The 1931
L 29 speedster-bodied Cord was a lower
longer version of its sister car, the Auburn Speedster.*
ABOVE: *810 Cord's instrument panel.*

small a slit for safety; its rear window was almost nonexistent.

The Cord 810, which appeared in 1936, was not E. L. Cord's first attempt at a front-drive car. In 1929 he had brought out an early F.W.D. machine, the L 29 Cord.

This L 29 used a straight-eight Lycoming engine of 125 hp, a solid front axle, and dual quarter-elliptic front springing. Its radiator shape and the lines of its front fenders were more than vaguely like those of its sister cars, the Auburn and the Duesenberg. This machine used early types of universal joint in its drive line, which ofttimes gave trouble. Further, its weight distribution was such that climbing slippery hills was sometimes a fairly chancy business, though not quite so tricky as the salesmen of rival makes made it out to be. This whispering campaign, a fairly high price ($3,095 and up), and the depression killed the L 29 in 1932, but not before 4,429 were sold.

In the fall of 1935 Erret Cord tried again with the Model 810. The independently sprung chassis, a new type of efficient universal joint, and a V-8 engine made the 810 a far better machine than the old L 29. But it was the new bodywork by Gordon M. Buehrig that bowled people over. The alligator hood, the unique horizontal louvres, the racy pontoon fenders, the concealed wind-out headlights made the new ultra-low Cord a sensation.

Oddly, Buehrig had first designed his revolutionary coachwork for a proposed Baby Duesenberg. As the Duesenberg project was nearing fruition, Buehrig was hastily called away to do some rush redesigning for Auburn, which was in dire straits. (Auburn's 1934 model had been a disaster.) After helping to pull Auburn out of its hole he went back to work on the Baby Duesenberg and was surprised to find that the brass had had some second thoughts. The infant Duesenberg was now to be a front-drive machine called a Cord.

But the lovely new Cord didn't sell too well, either. Although priced between $2,000 and $3,600, depending on the model, it was too expensive in a day when you could buy a big Buick for $885. In the two years of its existence fewer than 2,500 Cords were sold.

MERCEDES-BENZ

MERCEDES-BENZ Was, or is, the Mercedes-Benz a "great car"? It is impossible to answer that question. Over the years since 1885 or so, there have been very many Benz's and Daimlers and Mercedes' and Mercedes-Benz's. Some of them have been very great cars; a few have been perfectly awful cars.

Were this a history of Mercedes-Benz, I'd devote myself to the innumerable early tricycles and horseless carriages which Herren Daimler and Benz constructed before the turn of the century. But these devices were not yet the kinds of superlative motorcar with which Mercedes and Benz were to achieve fame. Daimler's and Benz's names would, in any case, have been everlastingly important for building the first self-propelled vehicles which we know actually propelled themselves, even if they had never built another car after 1890.

The first Mercedes car was, in a way, sired by one Emile Jellinek out of the Cannstatt-Daimler racing car of 1899. This Daimler-Phoenix-Wagen had been driven by Herr Jellinek, and he was no doubt deathly afraid of it. With good cause. It was a heavy little brute, high and short in wheelbase, and pointed in almost every direction except the way its driver wanted it to go. One of these devilish machines had already killed Wilhelm Bauer, the foreman of Daimler's Cannstatt factory. (The car pictured has had its wheelbase lengthened to improve its directional stability.)

Emile Jellinek had great influence with the Daimler Motoren Gesellschaft. He was the Austro-Hungarian consul in Nice and a director of the Crédit-Lyonnais, the French banking firm. More important, he was friends with the gilded community which gathered each winter on the Riviera, and not a man to let slip any financial advantages which might accrue from intimate acquaintance with princes, dukes, and mere millionaires. He sold them Daimler cars. He also frantically raced motorcars, a sport as fashionable at the time as, say, steeplechasing or pigeon shooting. And since it was also stylish not to use your own name while engaging in racing, he adopted the *nom du course* of Mercedes after his pretty daughter.

Jellinek wanted a better, safer car than that impossibly unwieldy Daimler-Phoenix-Wagen. He visited the factory at Cannstatt and proposed to Paul Daimler, Gottlieb Daimler's son, and to Wilhelm Maybach, the head designer, that an entirely new racing-cum-touring car be built. Sixty-six-year-old Gottlieb Daimler, ill with the heart trouble which soon would kill him, was not a party to these conferences.

The car which Wilhelm Maybach designed after these deliberations immediately made every other car in the world obsolete and ended the day of the horseless carriage. Jellinek instantly ordered thirty-six cars with the proviso that their name henceforth be Mercedes. Not long afterward he even petitioned the Austro-Hungarian emperor to change his name to Emile Jellinek-Mercedes.

The new *wunder-wagen*, with its four-cylinder, 5.32-litre engine was full of innovations. It was longer and lower than any other yet seen. It had a gear shift in a visible gate, control of engine speed by means of a throttle (most earlier engines had been controlled within narrow limits by means of spark adjustment or a governor which, if the engine ran too quickly, partly upset the exhaust valve action), and mechanically opened inlet valves which made control by throttle possible. Other car engines were still dependent on inlet valves which were opened

PRECEDING PAGES: 1929 *Model S 36/220-hp Mercedes-Benz, preferred by connoisseurs to later SS types. With lower radiator and hood, it is considered (except for its brakes) a more pleasing car to drive.*

London elegance in a German car. Henry Hewetson called this modified Benz a "Hewetson-Benz System." This photograph was taken in 1898. Note the candle lamp at the driver's right.

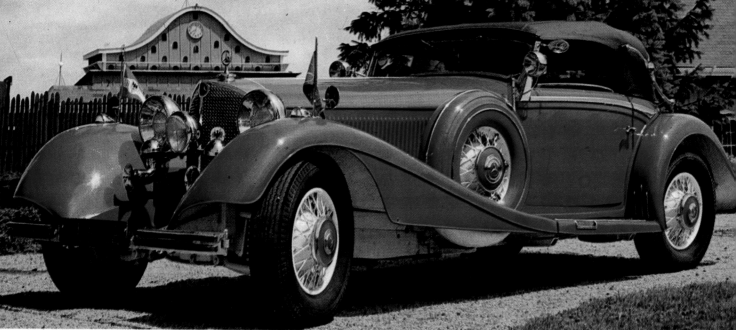

against springs by the suction of the descending pistons. Since these "automatic" valves operated correctly only in a narrow range of engine revolutions, it was almost impossible to slow the engine down without stalling it. Furthermore, the Mercedes had a honeycomb radiator which other makers quickly copied.

Rumors of the new Mercedes sent the world of automobilism into a tizzy of expectation, but initially there was a big letdown. Jellinek's nervous urgings had led the factory to ship the car by freight, untried and untuned, for its first tests in France. It behaved miserably, stripped its gears, jammed its bearings. Shipped again to its first race at Pau, it ran but a few yards before its clutch slipped and its gear lever stuck solid.

But when the factory mechanics at last got their revolutionary new baby into proper tune for the racing at Nice in March, 1901, it ran away from everything in sight, averaging 36.63 mph for 279.45 miles over the twisting and mountainous Estorel course near Nice. Try that on your 1967 Detroit bomb!

That was just a beginning. By 1903, the Daimler Motoren Gesellschaft was building one of the very greatest cars of all time, the fabulous Mercedes Sixty. It was listed as a "racing" car, but the term racing meant something rather different sixty-five years ago. Such a car was almost what we would call a sports car today. Fitted with gigantic goggling acetylene lamps and fenders, it was just the thing for haring around on the near-empty roads of the Riviera.

The Mercedes Sixty had what to our eyes would seem a huge, four-cylinder engine of 9¼ litres. Compared to the gigantic engines in its contemporaries, it was medium-sized. (The 70-hp Panhard-Levassor, for example, had an engine of 13.7 litres.) It had make-and-break ignition from a low-tension mag-

neto—a switch snapped open within the cylinder and produced the spark for igniting the charge. It was also possible to vary the valve timing and get lower compression for starting by means of a complex system of rods and gears. This gave more delicate control of engine speed than was possible by means of the carburetor throttle alone.

Such precise control was remarkable in its day and made gear-shifting a pleasure. No longer was it necessary to shift while an engine whirled away at a constant speed. Now with a quickly responsive engine it was possible to change gear for acceleration, for slowing at a corner. But I hasten to add that you couldn't drop down a gear and then, engine screaming, accelerate away like a shot. The Sixty developed its peak power at a mere 1000 rpm. By our standards, the Sixty's engine would seem rough and noisy. But at the time, A. B. Filson Young, in his book *The Complete Motorist*, wrote: "The perfection of the Mercedes engine is shown in its smooth and sure running,...and the clock-like steadiness with which the cylinders fire. If the silencer is cut out and the individual explosions of the exhaust are listened to, the sound is more like that of a very evenly worked Maxim gun than like the somewhat spasmodic throbs given out by less excellently designed and constructed machines."

Power from the engine was transmitted by a "scroll" clutch, a helical spring which gripped the drive shaft between engine and gearbox. Chains from the gearbox drove the rear wheels.

The rear-wheel brakes were internally expanding—also unusual for 1903—and at each application water from a special tank was squirted at the drums to cool them. A few years later Hispano-Suiza also used such a

133

TOP: *The* 1900 *Cannstatt-Daimler Phoenix racing car. Its wheelbase has been lengthened to make it less dangerous.*
CENTER: *A bulbous 1937 540 K convertible.*
BOTTOM: *Great Mercedes Sixty of 1903.*

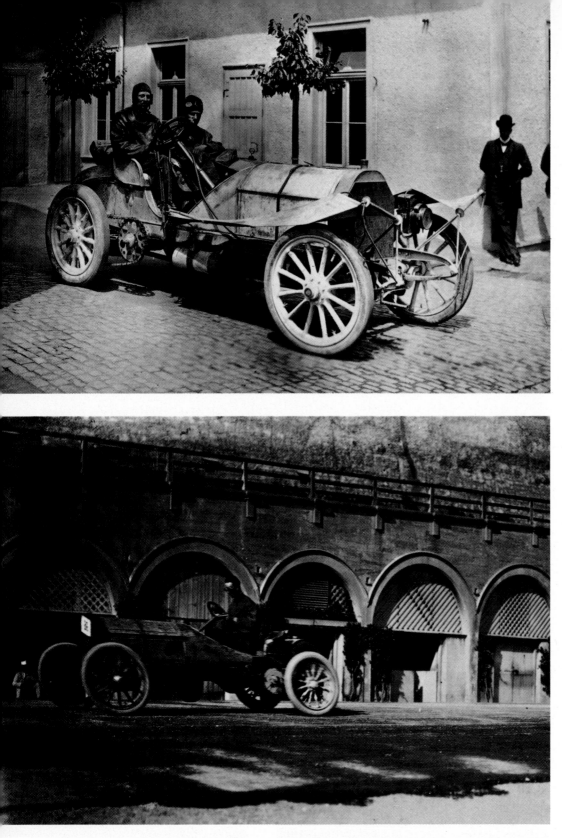

The red-bearded
Camille Jenatzy on 90-hp
Mercedes racing car
before 1904 Gordon-Bennett
race in Germany.
Jenatzy came in second.
Note front mudguards
made of canvas.

A 120-hp Mercedes
at the 1905 Brighton
Speed Trials in England.
Similar cars,
entered in the 1905
Gordon-Bennett
race in France, failed
due to tire troubles.
Cars were too
fast and too heavy
for 1905 tires.

FAR LEFT: 9¼-litre
four-cylinder engine of
Mercedes Sixty.
Original "make and break"
ignition has been
converted to use spark
plugs. LEFT: Cockpit of
the Sixty. Small
pipe organ affair is
multiple sight
feed lubricator. Array
of pedals includes
two for braking.

brake-cooling system.

On the road a Sixty gave its drivers a sense of untrammeled power, a feeling of godlike superiority. Drunk with their new-found ability to go fast—Sixties could reach 85—many a heavy-pursed young blood dashed himself to death on the boundary stones of an Alpine hairpin. Papa had to be very rich to buy his dear son a Sixty, which cost some $12,000—about $50,000 in today's money. It wasn't quite the car for daughter, however. She'd never be able to start the beast. Even young men had trouble cranking a Sixty engine and often left that onerous chore to the most gorilla-like groom in the family stables.

The Mercedes Sixty did uncommonly well in racing. Its most famous exploit was its win in the 1903 Gordon-Bennett race in Ireland.

A team of six 90-hp cars, basically similar to the Sixty, had been prepared for the race, but a catastrophic fire leveled the Cannstatt factory and destroyed five of the six Nineties. It was decided that the Sixties would have to run instead; they were very nearly as quick as the Nineties, anyhow. But there weren't enough Sixties quickly available. Clarence Gray Dinsmore, a rich American Mercedes enthusiast, offered the use of his car (we don't know exactly where the other two cars which made up the rest of the team of Sixties came from) and it was assigned to the red-bearded Camille Jenatzy, a diffident and quiet man who became a fiery demon behind a steering wheel. Dinsmore had used his car for touring and it was necessary to strip it of lights, fenders, and other amenities to get it down to fighting weight.

Jenatzy won the race and the Gordon-Bennett cup for the *Vaterland*. The other two Sixties, driven by Foxhall-Keene and the Baron de Caters, suffered various malfunctions and didn't finish.

During the next ten years, until World War I, Mercedes produced many cars of many models, most of them of the very first rank. Mercedes' were even, for a time, built by Steinway, the piano manufacturers, in Steinway, Long Island, not much more than a long bowshot away from the Simplex factory across New York's East River. These "American Mercedes'" were in every way equal to the German product. In fact, a Queens County-built, 70-hp model won three time trials at Ormond Beach, Florida, in 1907.

But what about the Benz?

If Carl Benz had been permitted to have his own way, the name Benz would not have helped to grace the radiators of today's Mercedes-Benz's. The name would very early have disappeared as a make of car and Carl Benz would only be remembered as a father of the automobile.

Carl Benz was an ultraconservative about cars and he liked the kind of old-fashioned gas buggies he had been building for years. While other makers were forging ahead with high-speed, four-cylinder engines and modern sliding-gear transmissions in cars capable of quite high speeds, Benz still clung to such things as rear-mounted, low-speed, horizontal engines and belt transmissions. In 1900 his cars generally differed but slightly from the Benz of 1890.

Benz cars sold quite well at first, especially in France as the Roger-Benz. They were well made—Benz detested anything that smacked of mass production—and they were reliable. But newer types of cars were rapidly putting the Benz company out of business. In 1900, for example, some six hundred Benz cars were sold, but by 1903, when other

TOP: 1921 28/95 Mercedes sports racer.
These supercharged cars did well in European racing and
hill climbs. In 1921 Sailer took
one into second place in the Targa Florio.

companies were booming, only one hundred and seventy-two left the factory. The Benz company directors were frantic and in 1902 hired a Frenchman, Marius Barbarou, to design a new line. Barbarou brought along his own French workmen to build the machines he designed, while another crew of Germans continued to build the archaic Benz. Barbarou's car, the Benz Parsifal, didn't pan out. In 1904, Barbarou went back to France and a young, new designer, Hans Nibel, was given the job. To Nibel must go the honor of making the name of Benz great, not only as that of a pioneer, but also as the producer of superb, modern motorcars. The royalty with which Europe was infested in those days started buying them, and Benz cars started winning in competition. In 1908, Fritz Erle, who became famous as a driver of racing Benz's, won on a 50-hp Benz that most important of early rallies, the Prince Henry "Tour," which was sponsored by Prince Henry of Prussia. (These Prince Henry Tours, which ran each year from 1908 to 1911, were more races than tours even though the competitors were required to have fenders, lights, and room for four passengers.) In that year, too, a 120-hp Benz driven by Victor Héméry won the St. Petersburg-Moscow race, a 430-mile run over atrocious roads. He averaged 51 mph, which meant he had to stay at 80 for much of the way over the chassis-breaking ruts and stones of the Czar's highway! A 51-mph average would be good even today—and the Soviets have since laid down a pavement. In July, 1908, Héméry on the 120-hp Benz showed Mercedes that they now had another German car to worry about. Only in the last few laps of the French Grand Prix was Lautenschlager, Mercedes' top driver, able to pass Héméry and take the lead. Héméry

was second.

But it is the fabulous Blitzen Benz which is most remembered from those years before the 1914 war. This 200-hp monster, designed by Nibel, first shocked the world of automobilism in October, 1909, when it came to the starting line at Brussels for the "World Championship," and perhaps shocked Mercedes even more by being 10 mph quicker than their invincible 1908 Grand Prix car.

In 1910 in the United States, the flamboyant, cigar-chomping Barney Oldfield first commenced his exploits with the Blitzen Benz by taking the world's flying mile record in 27.3 seconds at Daytona. The following year Bob Burman, also at Daytona, cut this time to 25.4 seconds—over 142 miles an hour—as fast as anyone had ever driven a car.

Up until World War I both Mercedes and Benz built numerous machines for touring and racing, almost all of the very first rank. But not until after Versailles and the marriage of Mercedes with Benz did they surpass themselves by offering anything as wildly blood-stirring as the twenty-years-gone Sixty.

In June, 1926, Daimler Motoren Gesellschaft and Benz & Cie. became one: Daimler-Benz Aktiengesellschaft. Henceforth the cars were to be called Mercedes-Benz.

The new company continued to build a line of bread-and-butter cars, as it still does. But now, too, using the talent of an engineering genius, Ferdinand Porsche, who had joined Mercedes in 1923, it started to lay down a line of the most delightfully brutal pantechnicons which ever thundered down a road.

Dr. Porsche had earlier designed the advanced and highly successful Austrian-built, overhead-camshaft Austro-Daimler. Later he designed the Auto-Union Grand Prix cars, the Volkswagen, and Panzer Kraft-Wagonen

137

The 1926 33/180 Model K supercharged
Mercedes-Benz. It was from this not-too-successful model
that Ferdinand Porsche later developed
the far better S type. The K was too high, too poorly
braked to cope with power developed.

for the tank divisions of the Third Reich. He also had more than a little to do with the layout of the 4CV Renault and, of course, the early Porsche sports cars.

In 1926 the first fruit of Porsche's labors, the 33/180, or Model K (for Kompressor), came forth. Unfortunately it was, in some ways, rotten. Its good points were meticulous finish and a fair turn of speed — over 90 mph, although 100 was promised by the factory. But only a hero driver would be addled enough to push one of those beastly K's up to even 90 mph. Its acceleration was, however, outstanding for 1926: 0 to 60 in twenty seconds. A friend of mine bought one, but not at its list price of circa $10,000. He got his used with practically no mileage on it (he found out later just why it had hardly been used) for $200 when it was only five years old.

Although my friend claimed that he got his bargain because of the depression which was then in full cry, I soon had no doubts regarding the K's first owner's anxiety to be rid of it.

The first time I was invited to ride in the K my friend lifted the impressively louvered hood with its cutout section to accommodate the curling, nickled outside exhaust pipes. I was suitably stunned by the monumental 6.2-litre overhead-camshaft engine *mit* supercharger, the Germanically thorough and accurate finish, and the Wagnerian rumbling which emanated from its bowels.

When, after the expected expressions of admiration, I finally climbed up and into the high seat next to the proud owner, I was honestly impressed. The long, long hood, the fierce swoop and howl of acceleration were heaven. But I returned from that ride, a shaken and aged youth.

Every fast corner was like Russian rou-

lette. On the straights at anything near 70 the K swayed and bounded from one side of the road to the other. We needed the whole width of the road and more. Worst of all were the brakes. Although purpled with the exertion of pushing down the brake pedal, the driver just couldn't make that *verdammte* K stop. At 40 mph you were lucky if you could halt within a two-hundred-foot New York City block. Still, many people liked the K. They drove it as if it were a 60-mph car, enjoyed the roar, and just talked about the 95-mph sports-car record Rudolf Caracciola set in one for the flying kilometer at Freiburg in 1926.

But Ferdinand Porsche took that miserable K and inside of a year made a great car out of it — the superlative S.

Porsche and the directors of Mercedes-Benz decided in 1927 that the best bet for increasing the prestige of their marque lay in sports-car racing rather than in Grands Prix, which were in the doldrums anyhow. So, waving his magic pencil over the drawing boards in Mercedes-Benz's offices, Porsche succeeded in making a silk purse, the S, out of that sow's ear, the K.

The new S, or 36-220 Mercedes-Benz, was one of those rare peaks in the history of motoring as the Sixty had been a quarter century earlier. The S was a superb sporting motorcar. Many connoisseurs of S series Mercedes consider it superior to its later versions, the various SS types, if only for its lower radiator, which made the whole car look less of a battleship.

It had a big 6.8-litre, overhead-camshaft engine which developed 120 hp at 3000 rpm. With its *kompressor* engaged it put out a thumping 180 hp, an awful lot of power for 1927.

Other cars of the period had super-

139

chargers, but that on the big Mercedes was unique. A Roots-type, it blew through the two Pallas carburetors (causing that beloved, ear-assaulting, scalp-lifting Mercedes scream, not unlike that of a lighthouse diaphone at close quarters). Other blowers on lesser cars were not quite so decibel-making since they sucked mixture from their carburetors before pumping it into the cylinders. Further, the blowers on other cars were spinning all the time. A Mercedes-Benz blower worked only when you wanted extra effort from the engine and tramped hard on the loud pedal. At that foot-on-the-floor instant a clutch engaged the supercharger. The factory discouraged overenthusiasm with the blower. No more than twenty seconds while accelerating, and never in low gear nor in high at top speed were the suggested limitations on use lest the engine be debilitated. I doubt, however, the lovely tale that continual use of the supercharger could cause the engine to macerate itself into bits small enough to exit through the exhaust system.

The engine and, in fact, the entire car was constructed and finished to almost unbelievably high standards of excellence. Light alloys were used to hold weight down, and although by no means a small machine, the S was quick on its feet. Steering was light and positive, albeit a mite heavy at parking speeds.

At its first public test on June 19, 1927, three Mercedes-Benz's appeared at the Nurburgring. One of them in the hands of Christian Werner was a full Grand Prix, eight-cylinder car. The other two, driven by Caracciola and Rosenberger, were the new S type sports cars. The sports cars proved to be faster than the Grand Prix car.

The new S, especially with Caracciola be-

hind the wheel, proved almost unbeatable in race after race. But Porsche and Mercedes didn't rest on their laurels. In 1928 new, faster versions of the S appeared: the 38-250 SS and the SSK (K for *kurz*—short). The SS had a 7-litre engine, a higher seven-to-one compression ratio, and more power—170 hp increasing to 225 hp with the *kompressor* cut in. The SSK, shorter and lighter and with more blower pressure, pushed out a hefty 250 hp. But the SSK was no longer entirely Dr. Porsche's baby. He left Mercedes in December, 1928, and Hans Nibel, who, you remember, had designed the Blitzen Benz, was responsible for its future development.

At the Nurburgring in 1928, the SS showed its stuff, coming in one, two, three against a gaggle of very quick Grand Prix Bugattis. Caracciola, of course, was first. In 1929 "Carratsh" actually had the nerve to drive a big SSK in that crazy "race of a thousand corners" through the twisting streets of Monte Carlo. If he hadn't been forced to change tires—due no doubt to some fancy sliding on the acute corners—he might have pulled it off. As it was he was only two minutes and thirteen seconds away from beating the ever-present swarm of Bugattis. He came in third.

The SSKL (L for *leicht*—light) was a lightened version of the SSK, drilled so full of holes it looked almost lacy. With its oversize "elephant" blower it developed about 300 hp. In 1931 Caracciola entered one in the wild figure-eight Italian Mille Miglia, which covered Italy from Brescia in the north to Rome in the south, crossing itself at Bologna. Caracciola drove single handed, averaged 95.8 mph on the 129-mile Brescia-Bologna stretch, and won, followed by a road-full of snarling Alfas and a pair of

O.M.'s. In the German Grand Prix of 1931, Caracciola, again pitting his sports car against an array of Grand Prix machinery, including factory-entered Bugattis and the great Nuvolari on an Alfa, brought his SSKL into first place.

How fast were these various S types? An S was capable of about 100 mph, an SS was some ten miles faster. An SSK would easily better 120 mph, while an SSKL, with a wind-cheating body and driven by Von Brauchitsch, at least once reached 156 mph! These cars were by no means cheap. An SS in 1934, for instance, cost about $15,000. An SSKL cost rather more if you could get the factory to part with one.

After the Germans embraced Adolf Hitler in 1933 Mercedes-Benz embarked, with government help, on a campaign to win in Grand Prix racing for the honor of the Third Reich. In this they succeeded. But now the character of the sporting Mercedes-Benz's changed. No longer were they the lean, clean, fast cars Dr. Porsche had envisioned. The production sports cars which took their place were the eight-cylinder, pushrod-engined 500 and 540 K's. They were fat and heavy (about 5,500 pounds) and vulgarly curvilinear. I thought at the time that if you had draped them with medals, they'd look like dear old Hermann Goering himself. If he'd had wheels. A good 540K, supercharger clutched in, would do 105 mph; 0 to 60 in about 14 seconds. (With blower it developed 180 hp; without, 115.) I ran away from one once in my old 4½-litre Invicta, but perhaps the Mercedes-Benz was in poor fettle that day. Still they sold well enough in this country—about $10,000—shipped with wooden tires to conserve rubber for the coming war. Up until a few years ago they were much sought after by collectors.

By 1945 the Mercedes-Benz factories which had helped power Hitler's Wehrmacht and Luftwaffe had been pounded flat by British and American bombers.

Daimler-Benz quickly climbed out of the rubble. By the fifties it was again a leader in Grand Prix and sports-car racing. Most of the cars built for sale have been prosaic, although well put together, and more than usually reliable family sedans and super-luxury cars like the 600, which was built for oil rich sheiks and Texans. But during the past fifteen years, Mercedes-Benz also has offered at least two outstanding machines: the slightly obese, gull-winged 300 SL sports car, which, although ofttimes tricky on corners, was very quick on its feet and did nobly in sports-car racing, and the current 230 SL, which is one of the nicest-handling sporting cars in the world today, if not the prettiest.

But if anyone were to ask me which among all the Mercedes' and Benz's and Mercedes-Benz's built since 1901 I'd choose to own, I'd be in a quandary. Would I pick a Sixty of 1903 or an SSK of 1929?

Mercedes still builds interesting cars in addition to thousands of family sedans it mass-produces. Below at left is the sporting 230 SL. At right, the huge and opulent 600, the Cadillac of Mittel Europa.

ferrari Many, if not all, of the motorcars discussed in these pages were greater cars in their youth than they are today. Although they may now be faster or more comfortable or easier to take care of, most have also succumbed to the attacks and the nasty little economies of the cost accountants who rule their makers.

The Ferrari is one of the very few machines whose builder still has some pride of mechanism, whose engine and chassis components are worth looking at for their own sakes. Certainly, even a Ferrari's machinery cannot be compared in accuracy and beauty of finish with, say, a prewar Bugatti or an Alfa Romeo. But even in a $14,200 Ferrari, costs must be held down to a degree. An eight-cylinder 2300 Zagato Alfa two-seater cost some $9,000 in the mid-thirties. A comparable Type 55 Bugatti was about the same price. Since money today will buy but a third of what it did then, a Type 55 Bugatti would cost almost $30,000 today. So you see, the Ferrari, being a sort of bargain, cannot offer you such luxuries as damascened firewalls or polished front axles.

If the Ferrari differs from those superb Bugattis and Alfas in the degree of its finish, it also resembles them in a most important way. Like the Type 55 Bugatti and the 2.3 Alfa, the current Ferrari sports types meant for use on the public highway are directly descended from the Ferrari racing cars.

And this is exactly what a real sports car ought to be—a de-tuned racing machine, not a warmed-over touring machine with a heavy, hotted-up lump of crudely cast iron under its hood, plus various makeshift alterations to its chassis meant to tone up the flaccid muscles of its suspension. Nor do trick stripes, the letters "GT," or sundry air scoops disguise its original advertised pur-

pose as a "personal car." Whatever that is.

I wish I owned a Ferrari, but I am lucky enough to have a few friends who do and who, upon occasion, allow me to conduct their admirable machines. I've driven a fair number of these, but not long ago I had the chance to drive one which I covet more than any of the others. This is a 275 GTB (Grand Turismo Berlinetta) owned by industrial designer John Cuccio, a man of rare taste in motorcars.

I was deep inside the ancient house in which I live. One kid had the television on, another was squealing into the telephone, my wife was issuing orders to still another. But a lovelier sound cut through this usual Sunday bedlam. It was the harsh, tingling music, the just-right sound of an engine that means business. I'm inured to hearing in my driveway the noises of almost any kind of car you can imagine, from the stumbling rumble of a sixty-year-old antique to the soprano of a small, modern sports car. But this car's stirring song had me out of the house like a rocket.

In the driveway stood the squat, vicious-looking, red Ferrari Berlinetta with Cuccio leaning against it, his elbow on the car's low roof. He held out the key. "Here, drive it," he said. What confidence! What friendship! Were the Ferrari mine, I'd *never* let anyone drive it.

I climbed in, one of my boys shot into the seat next to me, and we cinched up the seat belts.

Some years ago, setting off in a hot and uncivilized Ferrari would have given me pause. Its tricky clutch and crash gearbox would have occasioned a certain reticence. I'd have worried about breaking something. Turning the key, starting the 3.3-litre engine, and hearing that sudden, smooth

144

PRECEDING PAGES: *The
Ferrari is the race-bred machine.
Here Alberto Ascari
corners his 2½-litre Grand Prix
Ferrari at Monza in 1954.*

LEFT: *First Ferrari to reach United States was this 2-litre Type 125 imported by Briggs Cunningham in 1949. At wheel is George Rand.* BELOW LEFT: *1955 Pininfarina-bodied 375 Mille Miglia coupé.* BELOW: *Mike Hawthorne in 1958 at the Nürburgring.*

scream of power did make the roots of my hair prickle. But as I selected the lowest of the five gears and turned out of the driveway, I felt immediately at home. I found that I did have to use a gentle touch on the gas pedal if I didn't want the rev-counter needle to swing around in a blur or to spread rubber on the asphalt. After all, this car would go from 0 to 60 in a shade over 5 seconds.

I headed up the rolling, curving country road which passes my house and which is almost empty even on Sunday. In a sports car, on the short, straight stretches, 70 is normally about as high a speed as I reach, which is not bad. But today while still in third gear, my passenger nudged me and I glanced at the speedometer—90! Further on, now in fourth, I found myself touching 100 and having to force myself to slow down. And the disc brakes even made slowing a pleasure. It was uncanny, the car was so smooth, steered so perfectly, and had such snugly comfortable seating that speed meant just nothing. The scenery just went by a little more quickly—otherwise nothing. After enjoying this for some time, we decided to return by way of a wide turnpike. Pulling out to pass a slowpoke I forgot, for a moment, what I had under me and, still not in high, tramped momentarily on the throttle. My boy yelled, "Hey, Pop, you're doing a hundred and six in a sixty-mile zone." No wonder Cuccio collects traffic tickets. I'd like to make it clear, however, that such a Ferrari is much safer at 100 mph than a big, floppy, family sedan is at 50 — but not, perhaps, with a housewife at the controls.

This Ferrari was not the very latest 275 GTB. The newest type is called the 275 GTB4; the 4 indicates that it has four overhead camshafts, two for each six-cylinder bank of its V-12 engine. (Cuccio's car has a single camshaft over each bank.) The latest model also has six Weber carburetors and develops 300 hp at 8000 rpm. In fifth gear the factory claims a speed of 166 mph. Slap a number on its side and you can go racing in it. But don't imagine that's all it's good for. It's perfectly tractable for any kind of driving save, perhaps, the crawling from traffic light to traffic light we suffer in our cities.

There are other Ferraris you can buy. For example, the 330 GTC 2+2, a four-passenger "family" Ferrari capable of 150 or so. And the openable Spyder GTS which will reach a like speed and go from 0 to 60 in 6 seconds. And seen at European shows recently was the spectacular 365/P Berlinetta Speciale, a driver-in-the-middle three-seater with a rear engine.

The Ferrari is an unusual member of the nobility of automobilism. Its lineage doesn't stretch way back to the dear dim days; the first real Ferrari didn't take the road until 1947. The two eight-cylinder cars bearing the Commendatore's name, which were entered in the shortened Italian Mille Miglia of 1940, were not the true ancestors of the present line. The first typically twelve-cylindered Ferrari was the 1½-litre Type 125 of 1947. Designed by Gioacchino Colombo, who had been Alfa Romeo's chief designer, it had the features which have been part of almost every Ferrari ever since: an extreme, over-square V-12 with short con rods and light reciprocating masses revving at high speed. Only some of the racing machines have departed from the twelve-cylinder layout, which was retained in all sizes from 1½ to 5 litres. For twenty years now, although other makes — Mercedes-Benz, Maserati, even Ford — have briefly challenged Ferrari in sports-car racing, the marque still stands supreme, although it has been eclipsed on the Grand Prix circuits in recent years. Nor has any other make yet managed to replace it as *the* make to own as a prestige symbol for wealthy types who, unlike Rolls-Royce owners, wish to impress people with their youthful sportiness. Not so oddly, most Ferrari buyers are elderly parties over fifty.

Enzo Ferrari, like Ettore Bugatti, is a king in his own domain, his factory at Marenello in Northern Italy. No committees, no sales managers, no image makers pass memos around about what kind of cars to build. What Enzo Ferrari likes, Enzo builds. Period. Ferrari, now an imperious seventy, is no engineer but he has been car-crazy, racing-happy since he was a child. By 1918 he was working as a test driver. Then he got a job as a mechanic for Alfa Romeo. By 1923 he was a racing driver. Those were the great days of the P2 Grand Prix machines, the 3-litre, RLSS sports cars, and of drivers like Campari, Sivocci, and the elder Ascari. Ferrari was never a driver of the first rank. The P2's in Grands Prix were not for him, but he was fairly successful with the RLSS and its Targa Florio version, the TF in sports-car racing and hill climbs. The prancing-horse shield goes back to those days. Legend has it that after winning a race at Ravenna, a man and his wife presented him with the half-burnt shield cut from the fabric of the airplane in which their fighter-pilot son,

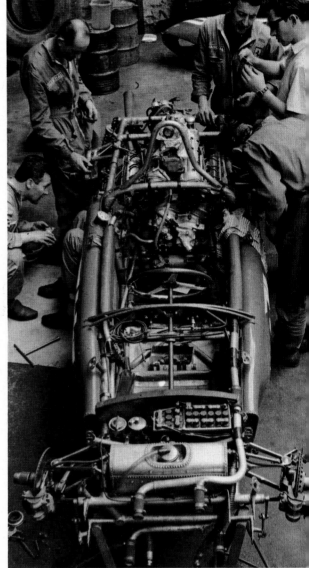

When British toppled Ferrari's Grand Prix supremacy with their
ultra-light, rear-engined racing machines, Ferrari had to follow new concept.
Classic front-engined machine (top left) gave way to rear-engined
cars like those driven by Phil Hill in 1961 (middle) and by Bandini in 1966
(bottom). ABOVE RIGHT: *1961 rear-engined Ferrari in the nude.*

Francesco Baracca, had died.

Ferrari was a better organizer than driver. Soon Alfa had him busy running its racing department and he seldom got a chance to race. Then Alfa gave up its own racing department and Ferrari set up the Scuderia Ferrari. Alfa built the cars, Ferrari hired the drivers, maintained the pits, directed the racing campaigns. Those years of the early thirties were Alfa Romeo's palmiest racing days. The great vans with the flying horses blazoned on their sides carried their racing machines from circuit to circuit, always winning. Famed drivers Nuvolari, Farina, Varzi left the deposed kings of Grand Prix racing, the Bugattis, in their dust. Then, as the thirties waned, the German Mercedes-Benz's and Auto-Unions started doing to Alfa as Alfa had done to Bugatti. Alfa Romeo, in 1938 under a new management which thought it could do better, formed its own racing Scuderia, Alfa Corse, and let Ferrari go. With results they must later have much regretted.

During the later years of the war, in his own small plant, Ferrari built machine tools, mostly for aircraft manufacturing. Bombed out, Ferrari rebuilt in 1946. Today the Ferrari factory's five hundred workers turn out only about one thousand racing and Gran Turismo cars each year, about three Gran Turismo cars a day.

That's one reason we can't all own Ferraris.

148

TOP: *Ferrari to come? In this rear-engined prototype, driver sits between his front passengers.* ABOVE LEFT: *1965 275 GTB Ferrari; 1967 version is 275 GTB4 with four overhead camshafts.* ABOVE RIGHT: *Since 1947, every Ferrari sold to public has been equipped with V-12 engine. This is 1953 version.*

*1956 4.9-litre Super America. Ferraris
change so slightly from year to year that a model of the late
fifties seems indistinguishable from a 1967. Their
kind of savage performance, though relished by the young,
is mostly bought by oldsters over forty.*

Simplex

Simplex

Some months ago I went to Ralph Buckley's Antique Auto Shop to see how he was coming along with certain mechanical and cosmetic refurbishments on a 1907 Welch with which I am romantically involved.

The Welch, which I hadn't seen for some months, as usual excited me, but equally if not more exciting was a 1910 Simplex Speed Car which was in the last stages of a magnificent restoration. Ralph Buckley doesn't merely reassemble and shine up an engine, and then run it briefly in the shop before he calls the owner to come get his car. He runs the cars he restores on the road, and for quite long distances. He listens for obscure ticks and squeaks. He adjusts timing and carburetion and a hundred other matters as he takes the car out again and again. I half suspect that these rides are as much fun as faultfinding.

Buckley was about to take the Simplex out again. "Want to come along?" he invited. It was cold out. The Simplex didn't even boast a windshield. I demurred.

Buckley tossed me the biggest bearskin coat I ever saw. It must have been built for a man eight feet high. Then he diddled with a few controls on the steering column and dashboard before walking to the front of the car.

I expected him to heave and grunt a bit as he tackled the crank. After all, a 50-hp Simplex has pretty big cylinders, 5¾-inch stroke *and* bore. But he had that engine so nicely in tune that I don't think he flicked the crank through more than 60 degrees of its circle before the giant four-cylinder T-head engine was booming away. I could feel each separate explosion through the soles of my shoes on the cement floor of the garage.

Buckley backed the Simplex out of the garage and into the road and I climbed aboard, lifting the dragging skirt of the bearskin.

You're really outdoors in a Simplex of that period. The low bucket seat seems yards away from the polished mahogany dashboard, the steering column as long as the post of a brass bed. And furry coat or no, it was cold out there. Buckley let out the clutch (all 67 plates of it), put the big outside gear lever into first, and we were off. He seemed not to steer at all—the wheel only took three-quarters of a turn from lock to lock. Once in high we flew along. The chains driving the rear wheels hummed loudly and musically. We were in heavy traffic but Buckley roared through it, steering the big Simplex in and out of the Detroit tinware as if it were some lower form of life to be ignored and passed by. Nothing passed us. At 75 we went by a couple of police cars parked at the roadside, but the cops just grinned and waved, surprising because Buckley hadn't even bothered to hang on license plates. Some years ago I had driven a similar Simplex with similar joy, tempered at that time by brakes that didn't seem to do much. But when Buckley was balked for a moment and hauled back on the outside lever (the foot brake on the transmission is for gentle retardation), the tail of the car seemed to squat and we slowed right down. No sweat there.

The 50-hp Simplex and the slightly more powerful 90, which had the same bore but a longer 6 1/10-inch stroke, were *the* great Simplexes, but there were earlier and later machines that were part of the dynasty.

Back in the early 1900's, when the young sports of Fifth Avenue and Newport bought big, expensive Panhards and Mercedes', they got them from Smith and Mabley, an elegant firm of car importers. But even in those

*Before 1907, the Smith and Mabley Simplex
had its own distinctive if ugly radiator design. Later,
when company changed hands, radiator
shape followed other cars in aping the Mercedes.
Note unusual oval headlamps—gas lit, of course.*

BELOW & RIGHT: *Pair of 50-hp Toy Tonneau Simplexes of 1911-1912. These fast 80-mph sporting machines had chain drive and big four-cylinder engines. Bucket-sized pistons were 5¾ inches in diameter. An even larger 90-hp engine was also manufactured. Odd davit-supported windshield on car at right was based on patented French device called* Pare-Brise Huillier.

RIGHT: *A tourer and a very formal town car from Smith and Mabley's 1906 catalogue, both of them photographed in front of New York's Hotel Navarre. Note chests of drawers under the front seats and exaggerated plowshare mudguards in front—a European touch.*

Three Simplex speedsters.
TOP LEFT: *The Smith and Mabley racing car entered
in the 1904 Vanderbilt Cup Race.* ABOVE:
Smith and Mabley sporting two-seater of about 1905.
TOP RIGHT: *Famous Simplex Zip racing car.*

income-tax-free days, $10,000 or $15,000 for a Sixty Mercedes or a posh Panhard was a lot of money, despite the fact that they were better cars than any built in this country.

In 1904, Smith and Mabley went into the car-building business because they reasoned that they could equal Europe's best at lower prices, minus a forty per cent import duty. The few Simplexes which survive for us to examine prove that they were the equal of almost anything from Europe and better than most. Until 1907, Smith and Mabley succeeded. In that depression year, like many other car makers, they failed, and a man named Herman Broesel bought them out.

Simplex's chief engineer and factory superintendent, Edward Franquist, didn't skimp. He used the Mercedes, at least partly, for his model and built his machines only of the very best materials: fine-grained "gun iron" for the cylinders and pistons, Krupp's chrome-nickel steel for the chassis frame, axles, and brake drums. He didn't trust outside suppliers even for such parts as rivets,

bolts, and nuts. In fact, except for wheels and tires and electrical mechanisms like magnetos, every part was made right in the little Simplex factory on East 83rd Street in New York. There, castings were poured, gears cut, dashboards and floorboards cut out, gas tanks soldered up. When the scalp-lifting uproar of unmuffled engines on test beds attracted inquisitive policemen, it was a simple matter to have someone invite them over to the corner saloon until they couldn't hear (or even see) too well.

The assembly line was a long wooden bench on which stood a half-dozen chassis. An expert fitter, a kind of man who has almost disappeared from our world, worked on each chassis, assembling the entire car from parts supplied to him. The company also provided a vise and a helper, but the mechanic brought his own tools. A good man could build an entire chassis in six ten-hour days.

When the chassis was finished, a box for a seat was mounted on it and a test driver would take it over to the wilds of Long Island and slam it around the rutted roads for hundreds of miles. When it got back to the factory, Franquist himself would take it out on test again before it went to the body builders, usually Healey and Co., J. S. Quinby, and later on Holbrook.

The Simplex was beautifully built, there is no doubt about that. But after fifty-five years or so, some slight faults have shown themselves. For example, no universal joint was fitted between engine and gearbox, so that there are strains on the transmission bearings when the flexible chassis frame weaves. The aluminum-alloy gear cases and crankcases are also showing signs of age. They're beginning to crack. The light alloys of fifty-five years ago weren't what they are today, and Ralph Buckley told me, with a straight face, that he doubted whether Simplex crankcases could stand another fifty-five years of use.

Like most sporting-car builders of the day, Simplex went racing, and quite successfully. To quote a Simplex catalogue: "On July 30 and 31, 1909, Simplex won the 24-hour race at Brighton Beach, New York, finishing 50 miles ahead of the nearest competitor in a field where the pick of American and European cars were found. On September 8, 1909, a 50-hp stock Simplex won the National Stock Chassis Race over the rough and tortuous Merrimac Valley course at Lowell, Massachusetts, covering the 318 miles in 352 minutes. Then came the clean-cut victory of a 90-hp stock Simplex chassis in the Founders Day Race at Fairmount Park, Philadelphia, on October 9, 1909, covering 200 miles of varied and difficult going in 218 minutes.... In the Brighton Beach 24-hour race of October 2-3, 1908 the Simplex was the winner, creating a world's 24-hour record of 1177 miles...."

But Simplex didn't mention an early racing failure back in the Smith and Mabley days when they built a special machine for Frank Croker, son of the Tammany boss, which he entered for the 1904 Vanderbilt Cup. This 75-hp monster couldn't make the regulation 2,204-pound weight limit. So they drilled it as full of holes as an Ementhaler cheese. During the race the filigreed chassis buckled so that the car finished with its innards dragging and making a triple track in the dirt of the road. With a new chassis at the Ormond Beach speed trials in January, 1905, the car rolled over, killing Croker.

In 1913 new owners—Goodrich, Lockhardt, and Smith—took over Simplex and moved the factory to New Brunswick, New Jersey. In 1914 they bought the Crane Motor Car Company of Bayonne, which had been making a big, top-quality, L-head, six-cylinder car, designed by a first-class engineer, Henry Crane. The Crane car was in the same price class as the Simplex (circa $6,000), but was a more refined, quieter, much less exciting machine. The thunderous old Simplex became the Crane-Simplex. During World War I the factory built thousands of those advanced aeroplane engines, the V-8 Hispano-Suizas, which late in the war powered the fighting Spads and Nieuports in their desperate struggle with the Germans. After the war Simplex became the property of an ex-Packard salesman, one Emlen S. Hare, and went down the drain when his company, Hare's Motors, went broke.

But, in a small way, the Simplex Company still exists. Famed collector, Henry Austin Clark, Jr., bought the name a few years ago. If you own a Simplex with one of those decaying crankcases, he's the man who can make you a new one.

156

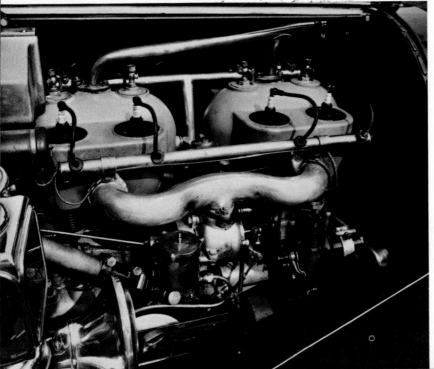

TOP: *Front view of 1912*
50-hp Toy Tonneau Simplex. Rear portions
of touring cars were usually
vast five-passenger "Tonneaus." When
shrunk in size for sporting
machines, they were called "Toy Tonneaus."
Note striking similarity of
Simplex radiator with that of Mercedes.

LEFT: *Clean and simple*
four-cylinder engine of 50-hp Simplex.

157

BUGATTI

BUGATTI The Bugatti was a motorcar. It had four wheels, a steering mechanism, seats, and an engine to propel it. But for the *Bugattiste* it has become a gilded calf, a graven image, a fetish, a juju. He venerates it as the totem of his religion. Why?

The reasons are not simple.

The Bugatti was the expression in metal of one complex, original, untrammeled genius, Ettore Bugatti. Some latter-day Bugatti worshippers have tried to make him out to be a lovable eccentric. That he was not. Bugatti was a benevolent despot. But so was Henry Royce and so were many of those other perfectionists who demanded that the cars they conceived be constructed *exactly* their way.

Therefore the Bugatti was different in the same way that one of Breguet's remarkable watches was different from every watch ever made. From its hollow, polished-steel front axle with its square apertures to receive the front springs (for many years Bugatti's technique for doing this was a mystery) to its quarter-elliptic rear springs a Bugatti was unique. A Bugatti engine, in its squarely architectural simplicity, looked like no other engine. Some enthusiasts find these engines so pleasurable to contemplate that they have meticulously rebuilt them to newness and display them as sculpture in their homes.

But a Bugatti didn't thrill by its look alone, by the delicate way it stood balanced on its wheels as if tensed for action. A Bugatti also went, and very quickly. And it had a blood-stirring feel and a sound all its own.

It wasn't until about 1930 that I became acquainted with Bugattis. I owned, at that time, a Model A Ford roadster. A friend owned a miserable machine, a high, narrow, Rosengart two-seater based on the Austin 7

and built in France under license. To get it serviced I went along with him to Zumbach's. There for the first time I saw a few Bugattis undergoing repair. I still haven't got over my breathless shock of delight. I found out that a dealer on the upper East Side had one or two Bugattis for sale and hurried to where he lay in wait.

He did have a couple, one a four-cylinder Type 40, the other a rather tatty blown eight-cylinder Type 43 roadster. Noting that I was drawn to the Type 43, he enthusiastically slapped the hood.

"This," he barked, "is just the car for a young fellow like you. Every time you leave the curb every one will think you're a great driver. Just wait and hear the noise it makes."

He jumped into the car, and started it. Its immediate response suggested that he had been expecting customers and had kept the engine warm. He drove it out of its space and backed it to the end of the aisle he kept clear between the rows of Isottas and Minervas and other such giants which were his chief stock. Then, in low gear, he shot down the aisle shrieking to a stop just short of the outside wall. He made it that day, but not long afterward the occupants of the nearby apartment houses were treated to the sight of a Bugatti's front end sticking out of a hole in the garage brickwork eight stories up.

I didn't buy that Bugatti because he wanted almost a thousand dollars. I regret it now, but the sum was beyond me. My friend, however, bought the little Type 40, which was fitted with a most peculiar two-seater body, rather like the chauffeur's compartment of a Coupé de Ville without the rear section where the boss sat. It was even possible to remove the leatherette front half of the roof, as on a town car.

I often rode in, and drove, this 1½-litre

160

machine—built about 1928, we thought. It was faster (about 75 mph) and had better roadholding than any car in our limited experience. But with the windows shut it was what I imagine riding inside a small metal-working factory would be like. It *was* noisy. At first the gear change at low speeds bullied us until we learned to fight back by just ramming the lever through. But we had one big problem: We could seldom get past 168th Street and Riverside Drive when going north out of the city. We'd make the mistake of obeying the "Hospital Quiet" sign there and tiptoeing on the accelerator. Immediately the plugs would oil and we'd be at the roadside juggling hot spark plugs. But getting your hands dirty is one of the prices you pay for the manifest joys of Bugatti driving. I've never gone on a trip in any Bugatti previous to the Type 57 where the tool kit didn't sooner or later come into play.

No, Bugattis are not easy cars to own and maintain. If you own one, you'd better teach yourself all about its mysteries. The mechanics to whom you can entrust your jewel can be counted on your fingers and, anyway, they're always busy with the disorders of other people's Bugattis. To do a carbon-and-valve job, for example, you must remove the cylinder block; the head doesn't come off. And in some models removal of the block requires the prior removal of the rear axle. On some early Bugattis, the Type 43, for example, the crankshaft's roller bearings are lubricated from oil jets set in the side of the crankcase which receive their oil through skinny copper tubes. A curl of lint can block a pipe with disastrous effect. So if you're a dedicated *Bugattiste,* you don't go near a disemboweled engine with a rag. A camel's hair brush is more nearly the correct instrument. And on those models with wet clutches you'd

better learn exactly how to adjust things, and exactly what mixture of kerosene and oil to administer, if you want the clutch to function without stubbornly refusing either to release or to grip at all.

The most painful case of a Bugatti's malaise in which I was involved had to do with a Type 51 Grand Prix car which I owned with a friend. We had bought it after the 1936 Vanderbilt Cup race where, in practice, it had poked a rod through its crankcase.

We had it hauled to Zumbach's for dismantling and cure. The exploratory operation showed a much-mangled rod, a hole in the aluminum crankcase, plus evidence of earlier rod exits, and a scored and blued journal on one of the segments of the come-apart crankshaft. (The crankshaft was made in pieces to allow the roller bearing rods to be slipped on endwise.) Zumbach's mechanics took the shaft apart and we shipped the bits to the Bugatti factory at Molsheim in Alsace for identification and replacement. In a few months a new connecting rod and bearing and a new section of crankshaft arrived looking like jewelry in a lovely wooden box. Zumbach's put things back together. The engine sounded fine—fine being a combination of the calico-tearing and crackling sound of the exhaust, another noise like a stockroom full of small metal parts going down a tin chute, plus the whining and growling of the supercharger. Alas, one morning soon afterwards my friend stood on the gas pedal to race a Chevrolet out of a toll booth. And the same rod emerged again. The car was sold as is. Its new owner installed a Peerless marine engine, of all things.

Imagine you have, say, a Type 55 (eight cylinder, twin-overhead camshaft, 2.3 litres) in your garage. It's December and pretty cold. Do you just swing up the garage door,

161

II GRAND PRIX AUTOMOBILE DE MONACO

ABOVE: *Type 35B 2.3-litre supercharged Bugatti made from 1927 to 1930. Types 35 were most successful Bugatti racing machines. This one is equipped for road use.*

LEFT: *Most of the cars starting in the 1931 Monaco Grand Prix are Type 51 Bugattis. The other cars are Maseratis and Alfa Romeos.*

RIGHT: *Dignified architecture of the straight-eight supercharged 2.3-litre Type 35B engine. Blower is at the bottom of the photograph.*

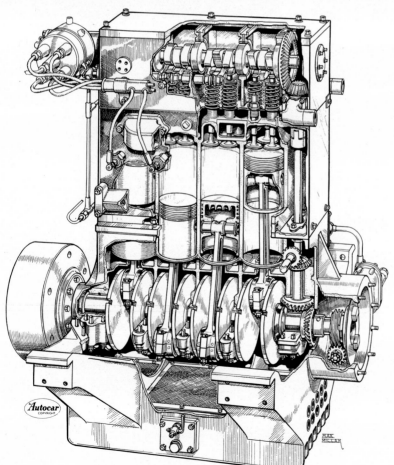

ABOVE LEFT: *Front aspect of a 2-litre unblown Type 35 Bugatti. The lovely hollow front axle was originally of polished steel, but modern restorers plate the lily with chromium. Lights and fenders are also recent changes.*

ABOVE RIGHT: *Cockpit of Type 35 Bugatti. Bosch magneto protrudes through instrument panel. Lever to its left is ignition control. Note that this Grand Prix car is a two-seater; single-seaters came later.*

LEFT: *Max Millar drawing of Bugatti four-cylinder Type 37 engine. Single-overhead camshaft operates three valves per cylinder. Note disc-webbed, five-main-bearing crankshaft. Holes in end of crankshaft are ends of oil-cooling tubes.*

settle yourself in the seat of the Bugatti, press the starter, and embark for the Sea Horse Bar and Grill?

Chances are the Bugatti won't start. If you're an initiate in the rites of *Bugattisme,* you drain out the water and refill with new, clean, preferably distilled or at least filtered, hot water. You drain the crankcase oil into a clean container, warm it on the kitchen stove, and replace it. You still don't brutally use the electric starter. First you hand crank the engine with the switch off to unstick the pistons from the congealed, adhesive oil in the cylinders. *Then,* you use the starter. And if your darling's engine clatters into action, you sit there letting it warm for ten minutes at 1000 rpm. Idle that long at a slower speed and you'll oil the plugs. Ettore Bugatti knew whereof he spoke when he advised people griping about hard starting to keep their cars in heated garages.

Is a Bugatti worth all this fuss? It certainly is if just looking at a lovely, ingenious mechanism gives you joy, if you appreciate a motorcar which goes exactly where you direct it, which is nervously alive and an extension of your hand and brain.

Ettore Bugatti was a Milanese, born in 1881. His artistic family wanted him to continue the family tradition and he was sent to study sculpture. Bugatti never did become the kind of artist his family wanted him to be. Rather he became an artist in metal, in the inspired shapes of his motorcars.

In the late 1890's, when Bugatti was seventeen, he became infected with the new excitement over motor vehicles. He bought a motor tricycle and left his art studies to become an apprentice at the engineering works of Prinetti and Stucchi. After a year, and in spite of never having any formal engineering or technical schooling, Bugatti started building himself a motor vehicle—a twin-engined tricycle—the first in the line of remarkable machines he was to construct during the next forty years.

Bugatti established his own factory in 1909, at Molsheim in Alsace. At twenty-eight he was already a famed automotive designer and had used his talents toward furthering some of the great makes of Europe: De Dietrich, Duetz, Mathis, Peugeot.

Bugatti's "factory" was hardly the usual greasy, noisy *usine.* It was a small principality ruled by a benevolent prince. The production of distinguished motorcars was just one of its functions, albeit the most important. Bugatti was fanatically interested in horseflesh and maintained baronial stables. *Le pur sang,* the pure blood, was a term he applied to his cars as well as his horses. He was a connoisseur of great wines and grew his own vines. He even established an inn for customers coming to collect their cars.

In thirty years fewer than seven thousand cars, about five each week, were produced. Many of the thirty-six different models were racing machines, notably the straight-eight Type 35, which first appeared in 1924 and which in its various forms, from the unblown 1½-litre Type 35 to the supercharged 2.3-litre 35B, won more races than any racing cars of all time. In 1925 and 1926 alone they won over a thousand times!

There were, over the years, other racing types, although none was so brilliantly successful as the Types 35. Noteworthy among these was the four-cylinder 1½-litre Brescia (named in honor of a one, two, three, four victory at Brescia in 1921), which soon after World War I began to make Bugatti a great name on Europe's racing circuits and hill climbs. It was on Brescias that British drivers

ABOVE: *1932 5-litre Type 50 Bugatti with Carrosserie Profilée coachwork. 110 mph was possible with impeccable handling.*

RIGHT: *Front aspect of Type 50 Bugatti. Note how cutaway fenders allow view of beautiful axle, springs, and brake drum.*

OPPOSITE PAGE, LEFT: *Front brake, finned aluminum wheel, and polished axle of Type 50. Shocks were adjustable from cockpit.*

OPPOSITE PAGE, RIGHT: *Type 50 was first Bugatti to have twin-overhead-camshaft engine. Two carburetors were below supercharger.*

Type 30, 2-litre Bugatti, built from 1922 until 1926.
It had a straight-eight engine with twin carburetors. This one with doorless
body is called "the toast rack" by its British
owner. While Type 30 was not one of Ettore Bugatti's best efforts,
several racing machines were based on it.

Henry Segrave and Raymond Mays and France's Louis Chiron first gained fame.

Another was the G.P. Type 51 of 1931, the first Bugatti racing car with twin-overhead camshafts operating the inclined valves of its 2.3-litre supercharged engine. The Type 51 also had two derivates: the 51A, a 1½-litre machine, and the 2-litre 51C. (Since 1927 and the Type 35B, most Bugatti Grand Prix cars had superchargers, but Ettore Bugatti never liked them, considering forced induction as somehow not cricket.)

The huge, 5-litre Type 54, which dates from 1932, was one of Bugatti's failures. Designed and built in two weeks, it turned out to be surprisingly unroadworthy for a Bugatti. Although some 54's won a few races —Achille Varzi took first place at Berlin's Avus track in 1933 at 128.48 miles an hour —a Type 54 also took the life of Czaykowski on that terrible day at Monza in September, 1933, when Campari's and Borzacchini's Alfas skidded on oil and killed them.

In 1933, the Type 59 Grand Prix car appeared, first in twin-cam, straight-eight, blown 2.8-litre form. Then, in 1934, since it was not quite fast enough to contend with the Alfa Romeos, its capacity was increased to 3.3 litres. By then the German Auto-Unions and Mercedes' were defeating the Alfas, and the 250-hp, 175-mph Type 59's still were not quick enough to win. The Type 59 was as beautiful a race car as Bugatti ever built. In a day of independent suspensions it still retained that lovely Bugatti trademark, the polished front axle. Although the axle was split on its center line the two halves were joined by a knurled collar; Bugatti believed that the split axle somehow gave a degree of independent suspension. The 59's wheels looked like wire, but really weren't. The weight of the car was taken on

what amounted to a polished disc, the radial wires serving mostly to locate the hub.

Many of Bugatti's touring machines closely followed the design of the racing cars of each period. The touring version of the Brescia, called the *Brescia Modifié,* was a racing car detuned and simplified for road use. Similarly, the Grand Sport Type 43 of 1927 was a beefed-up and longer-chassised version of the 35B racing machine. I think the Type 43, with a standard pointed-tail torpedo body, is still my favorite among Bugatti road cars. Its blown 2.3-litre, single-overhead-camshaft engine makes an awful lot of noise for the 120 hp it develops. Its ride is harsh. It's impossible to service. But it has the true stark Bugatti look. It has that inimitable Bugatti chassis with ridiculously delicate goosenecks gradually thickening to a deep section in the vicinity of the firewall. It not only has quarter-elliptics aft, but they show nakedly, as every other exciting bit of Bugatti anatomy shows on this model. And no Bugatti I've ever driven has quite the wild feel of a Type 43 at full bore, even though its top speed, about 110, isn't much by today's standards.

I still feel pangs about three, spanking new Type 43's, one of them with a white Grand Sport torpedo body, the others with dark blue, convertible coachwork, which sat for sale in a window on Park Avenue and 47th Street in New York. It was, I believe, in 1931 or 1932 and the $1,500 prices were too high for me. I think that these were the three cars which "le Patron" traded to American driver Leon Duray for the twin-cam Miller-engined "Packard Cable Specials." Much later I saw the white Grand Sport in Zumbach's for rebuilding. It was a pretty sorry sight. Its tobacco-heir owner had left it out in the weather for years and

169

appreciative chickens had roosted in it.

Bugatti's study of the twin-cam Miller engines resulted in his twin-cam Type 51. The sports version of the Type 51 was the Type 55 of 1932. This had the 2.3-litre blown Type 51 engine in a heavier Type 54 chassis, and was one of the very great sports cars of all time.

There were other big, fast, de luxe Bugatti types in those years between the war. One was the giant 5.3-litre Type 46 and 46S (supercharged) of 1929. The 46's were favorites of Monsieur Bugatti, if not of some American mechanics who had to work on them. This was the model with its three-speed gearbox in the rear axle, the one whose rear end had to be removed if major engine work was needed. Although capable of 90 or so, the 46 was more the de luxe carriage than it was a sports car. The Type 50 of 1930 was another luxury car similar to the Type 46, but with a twin-cam 5-litre blown engine. It was faster, too. Close to 110 mph was possible.

Bugatti built even more sedate touring machines. The quiet (for a Bugatti) Type 44 of 1928—"the Molsheim Buick"—and a later, similar machine, the Type 49 of 1930. The Type 44 had a 3-litre single-cam engine, the Type 49 was slightly enlarged to 3.3 litres. Surprisingly, although you might imagine that anyone wanting a Bugatti would buy as hot a one as he could get, it was the cool Type 44 that had the biggest sale of all Bugattis. More than 1,200.

On occasion, Ettore Bugatti could think big, very big. In 1927 the incredible, gigantic Type 41 Royale, the Golden Bug, appeared. M. Bugatti is supposed to have produced this imposing behemoth for the use of kings, but not even the least important of backwoods Balkan monarchs bought one. At

$30,000 for the chassis alone, it was most likely too expensive. The overhead-camshaft engine had a 13-litre capacity, 300 hp was developed at 1700 rpm. The wheelbase was 169 inches, the track 66 inches. The outside diameter of the tires was 40 inches. Only six or seven or so of these majestically overgrown devices ever were built, although engines of the same specification were later installed in the Bugatti "automotrices," the rail cars. Bugatti had a sense of humor. He supplied a white elephant radiator ornament for each of these grandiose machines.

The last Bugattis to go into series production were the various models of the Type 57. The first 57 Normale with its 3.3-litre, eight-cylinder, twin-overhead-camshaft engine caused rude remarks about "twin-cam, Type 44 Molsheim Buicks," but the 57 was no Buick, especially as Bugatti began bringing out more puissant versions: the 57C (supercharged), the 57S with a lower chassis and higher compression, and finally the 57SC, perhaps the finest all-round sporting machine of all time, which had the low chassis *and* supercharging.

In 1936 a standard 57S—*un*supercharged—covered a distance of 135.4 miles in one hour at the old Montlhéry Autodrome near Paris. In 1937 and again in 1939 similar cars won at Le Mans.

In 1940 the Type 57 went out of production, forever. The factory suffered from the Germans, the Canadians, the Americans. Just before the war a prototype for the Type 64, a car to replace the Type 57, had been in the works. It had a light alloy chassis, a twin-ohc (chain driven), 4½-litre engine with twin downdraft carburetors and a Cotal electric gearbox. During the war Bugatti developed, for postwar production, a tiny, two-seat roadster with a 370-cc over-

This Type 57 of the late thirties has a body
which is unusual for a Bugatti. Flamboyant coachwork is by Saoutchik, whose
work is more usually seen on plushy Delages and
Delahayes. Note the extremely shallow windshield and the clock set
into the un-Bugatti-ish steering-wheel hub.

TOP LEFT: *Driver's compartment of Type 57C Bugatti.
Note simple steering wheel and long, whippy gearshift lever.*
ABOVE: *3.3-litre twin-cam supercharged engine of the
Type 57C.* TOP RIGHT: *A 1939 Type 57C Atalante coupé by Gangloff.*
RIGHT: *1932 Type 55 Super Sports, Bugatti's greatest sports
car, had same 2.3-litre engine as Type 51 Grand Prix car. Driver sits
comfortably upright with his feet in deep wells.*

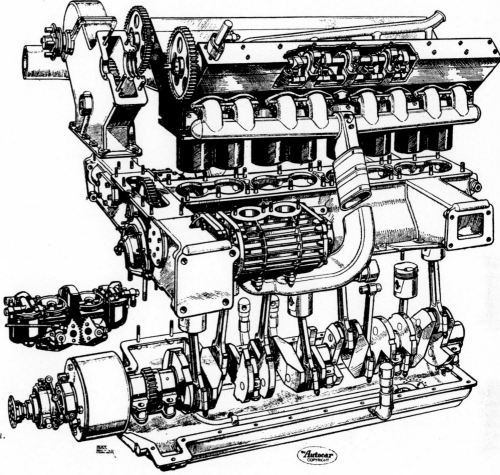

TOP LEFT: *Gargantuan Type* 41 *Bugatti Royale had* 12,763-*cc engine, wheels* 36 *inches in diameter, and was only slightly less than a quarter mile long. No royal buyers turned up for $30,000 car.*

CENTER LEFT: *Front elevation of a Type* 57SC, *most powerful and quickest of Types* 57. *Its blown engine developed* 220 *hp and top speed of* 135 *mph. Last year for this and* 57S *was* 1938.

BOTTOM LEFT: *Last of the Bugattis? This Type* 101 *built after World War II differed from Type* 57 *in having chain- instead of gear-driven overhead camshafts. Cotal electric gearbox was standard.*

RIGHT: *Exploded view (by Max Millar) of the* 3.3-*litre engine of Type* 59 *Grand Prix Bugatti. Note (at left) geared-together throttles of twin carburetor. Engine developed* 260 *hp at* 6000 *rpm.*

head-cam engine, the Type 68. In 1946 Bugatti was engaged with various touring and racing, blown and unblown, versions of a four-cylinder, 1½-litre car, the Type 73. In fact a Type 73 chassis was shown at the 1947 Paris salon.

But Ettore Bugatti was already gone by then. He had died a few weeks before, on August 21. None of his postwar projects ever reached fruition.

In 1951 at the Paris salon a new car bearing the red Bugatti oval was shown. This,

the Type 101, was basically the Type 57 with slight modifications. It had Weber carburetors, slab-sided bodywork, and seemed to be a very fine motorcar. Somehow it never got into real production. (But only a few weeks ago I saw one streaking down the Connecticut Turnpike.)

A Grand Prix Bugatti with a transverse 2½-litre engine appeared fleetingly in 1955.

Ettore Bugatti has been gone for twenty years. I'm afraid we had better stop hoping for a new car bearing his stamp.

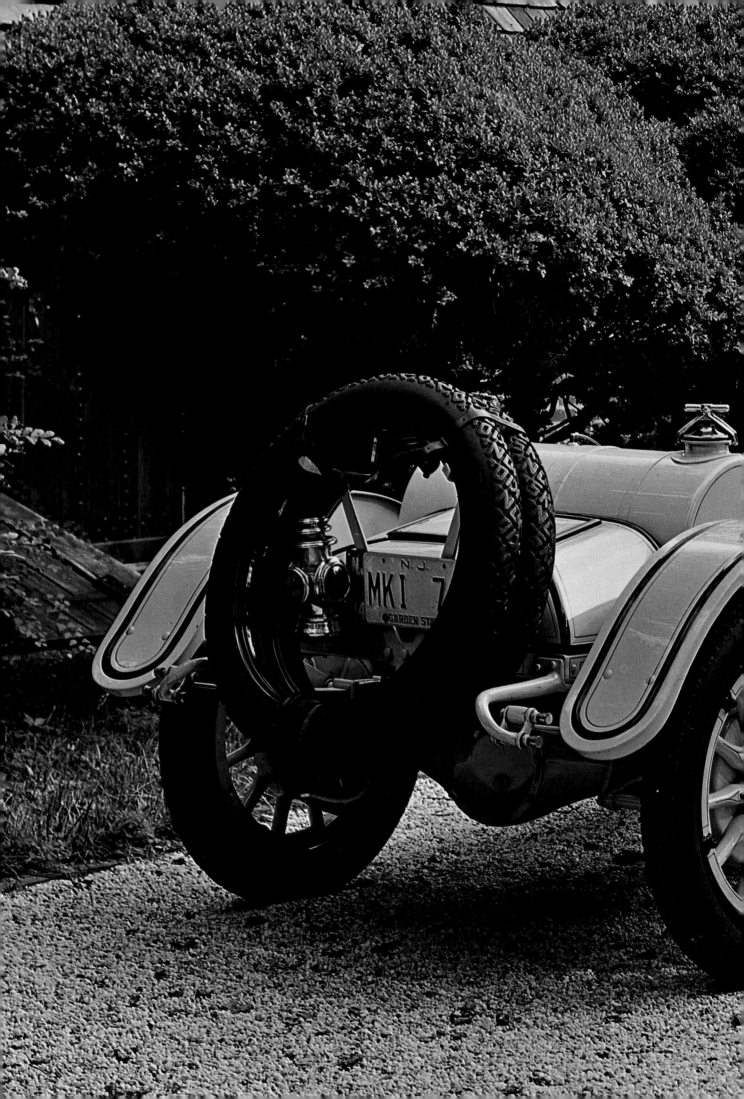

MERCER

PRECEDING PAGES: *The collector's dream, a 1914 Type 35
Mercer Raceabout.* ABOVE LEFT: *The 1910 Mercer Speedster, antecedent of
Raceabout.* ABOVE RIGHT: *Monocle windshield of
the 1914 Mercer Raceabout.* LOWER LEFT: *Front wheels were visible
from cockpit.* LOWER RIGHT: *Front wheel hub of 1914 Mercer.*

MERCER

Half a dozen years ago, in a book about automobiles, I wrote a gee-whiz sentence: "Ralph Buckley told me recently that at least one oil-rich Texan has been offering $10,000 for a nice Raceabout, with no takers." Those "no takers" had rather more vision than I did, for a T-head Mercer Raceabout of about 1912 is today worth several times $10,000. Not too long ago, a New Jersey man I know invested $31,000 in such a car and, unless our economy goes bang, a Raceabout may well be worth $50,000 in a couple of years. Raceabouts are like Rembrandts; nobody is turning them out these days and there are very few of them around. Also, like Rembrandts, it is not only their rarity that makes them so valuable—there are rarer cars and rarer paintings—but their sheer desirability.

Why *is* a Mercer Raceabout so desirable? First, I suppose, is its look. Of course, there were many other sporting cars built in the same idiom. Built for speed and amusement, they dispensed with everything except an engine and a chassis, a container for fuel, and two perches upon which the conductor and his accomplice sat. Stutz built such cars. So did Fiat and Mercedes and Isotta-Fraschini and National and Marion and Simplex. We could write out a long, long list. Somehow, by chance or design (I suspect it was chance), the components of a Mercer were arranged on a chassis rather lower than the ones I've mentioned so that they looked just right. By comparison a Stutz Bearcat, for example, looks gross and clumsy. A Raceabout's fenders have exactly the right sweep and curvature. Its steering column, surmounted by a monocle windshield, can't be tilted a half inch either way without destroying the car's look. But as with the Raceabout's other functional parts

—the angles of the brake and shift levers, the relation of the seats to the rear wheels—it wasn't "styling" that decided on angles and placements, it was merely that the car worked best that way. I once asked the late Mr. Finley Robertson Porter, who designed the Mercer, how the appearance of the Raceabout was arrived at. "Why, we just built it that way," he said. Mr. Porter didn't know about such exotic creatures as stylists until forty years after his cars took to the road.

But a T-head Mercer Raceabout doesn't merely look great. It goes that way, too. Assume it's a fine May morning, and you prevail upon your wife to accompany you on a run over the narrow back roads in the countryside near where you live. (If you own a Mercer Raceabout, you move to the country, and preferably have a wife who likes sitting outdoors in a hurricane.)

Starting a Raceabout is no different from the drill you go through with any pre-self-starter machine. You set gas and spark levers, and perhaps inject a few drops of fuel into the cylinder petcocks, etc., before you address yourself to the hand crank. If your engine is in good fettle, it starts booming away with no fuss after a turn or two.

You have to get into the car from the left; the shift and brake levers block right side entrance. You brace your foot against the brass stirrup which lives outboard of the chassis so that your toe can manipulate the accelerator pedal, a sort of bent brass spatula which is outside the cockpit. I shouldn't use the word "cockpit," which implies a degree of enclosure, for there is no enclosure; you're as much outside as if you sat on the forward edge of the wing of a 1909 Curtiss biplane.

The Raceabout is surprisingly easy to drive. The big-toothed gears could be shifted by an old lady used to manipulating those

on a Volkswagen. And you can, if you like, drive a Raceabout in the same way that most machines of its day were driven, by immediately going through the gears (three before 1912, four thereafter) into high and staying there.

At first, this May morning, you drive like that. Slowly and sedately you loaf along so that you can almost hear each separate explosion (you have the cutout open). The road climbs and twists, a couple of youths in the family sedan wallow past, sniggering. You drop into second, roar up on their tail, and go by at the first straight stretch. A Mercer Raceabout is a pretty potent machine in second. The road starts twisting again so that the kids have all they can do to stay on it, let alone catch you. For the Raceabout steers like a sports car. If there's a bottle cap in the road, you can choose whether to steer so as to touch it with either the inside, the outside, or the middle of your tire tread. Being able to watch the right front wheel helps.

The Mercer Raceabout has its faults, too. It was never worth a damn for a longish trip; few people can stand the buffeting of the wind very long. Even the driver, with his monocle windshield, gets pretty windblown. Further, a Raceabout's brakes, although adequate for the traffic-less roads of 1912, are hopeless today. You have to plan to stop a long way ahead and then haul back on the handbrake. The foot brake, gripping the drive shaft, is for checking speed, not stopping.

The Mercer chassis were light, and over the years have shown a certain fragility. The chassis of almost every Mercer around today has been cracked and rewelded with reinforcing gussets. Engine and transmission bearers tend to crack, too. But it must be remembered that most Mercers have lived a hard life. Generations of young hellions got hold of them and they were racketed around over rough roads for years after their original owners sold them.

The Mercer was built in Trenton, Mercer County, New Jersey. In 1909, members of the Roebling family (the Brooklyn Bridge Roeblings) and some people named Kuser embarked upon the manufacture of motorcars, especially of sporting character. Their first car was the Model 30-C Speedster. Low and tough and with a four-cylinder Beaver engine, it already had some of the character which was to reach full bloom in the Raceabout two years later. But along with the sporting cars other types were also built: tourers, even limousines with the L-head Beaver engines, and some with Continental engines.

When, in 1911, the Type 35 Raceabout was born, it had a four-cylinder, 300-cubic-inch (5 litre), T-head engine, a wet multiple-disc clutch, and during its first year or so, a three-speed gearbox supplied by Brown and Lipe. A mile in 51 seconds was guaranteed by the factory, but they were being conservative. Some Raceabouts were much faster, especially those whose owners meant to race them and modified them by drilling the skirts full of holes to lighten the pistons and by cutting down their heavy flywheels.

But stock Raceabouts brought from the showroom floor to the racecourse, like Bugattis fifteen years later, could race and win, too. In 1912 Spencer Wishart did just that. After buying a stock Raceabout he proceeded to the track at Columbus, Ohio, and won himself a 200-mile race. Not only that—he set four track records for various distances. Many of the crack drivers of the day used racing versions of the Mercer with

The L-head Mercer appeared in 1915. Designed by
Erik H. Delling, it was heavier than the old T-head Raceabout,
but had more power—70 hp vs. 50 hp for the earlier
machine—and was somewhat faster. Factory guaranteed a mile in
48 seconds. By 1919, L-head Mercer even had a windshield.

450-cubic-inch engines, bigger than the stock 300-cubic-inch Raceabouts. Ralph DePalma, Barney Oldfield, and Eddie Pullen all at one time or another drove Mercers. In 1912 Ralph DePalma won the 300-cubic-inch class in the Santa Monica, California, road race. He *averaged* close to 70 mph for the 150 miles. In 1914 the great Eddie Pullen won the 301.8-mile Corona, California, road race at 87.76 mph.

Mr. Porter left the company in 1915 and a different kind of Raceabout came into being. Designed by Erik H. Delling, it was perhaps a more civilized motorcar, but a somewhat less exciting and desirable one. Although the official designation of the new machine was the 22-70, no one today calls it anything but the L-head to distinguish it from the T-head.

The engine of this new Raceabout had about the same cubic capacity as the older T-head — 298 cubic inches. It had what seems to our eyes an unusually long stroke, 6¾ inches with a bore of 3¾ inches, which caused it to use long, skinny, 15-inch connecting rods. The 22-70 tag meant that it had 22 hp on formula and 70 actual brake hp at 2800 rpm. L-head enthusiasts claim as much as 90 bhp at 3000 rpm, but I should think that the long rods and the thinnish, three-bearing crankshaft might engender some concern at high revs.

This new car had doors, electric starting and lighting, left-hand drive, and a central gear lever sticking out of an unconscionably big ball joint on the floor. By 1919 the Raceabout had become so effete as actually to have a factory-installed windshield.

I hasten to say that although I think the L-head lacked some of the brutal charm of the T-head, it was still one of the very great sports cars and it was a more practical car

for longer journeys. And according to the factory, it was faster than the old T-head. They guaranteed a mile in 48 seconds in spite of the fact that the L-head was heavier (3,500 pounds vs. 2,850 pounds).

Mercers in several forms, including touring cars with six-cylinder engines, were made until the mid-twenties. By 1918 the Roeblings, who had guided the company, were dead. A Wall Street combine got control of still-healthy Mercer and put at its head Emlen S. Hare, the same gentleman who had taken over Simplex. By 1923 Mercer was in receivership, by 1925 dead.

There was, about 1930, an attempt to revive the great Mercer name. A new company called Mercer Motors Corporation of Elkhart, Indiana, showed a few demonstration cars based on a defunct make, the Elcar. These machines, really Elcars with Mercer shields on their radiators, had eight-cylinder engines, hydraulic brakes, etc. But that effort, coming as it did in the desperate days of the Hoover administration, was doomed from its start.

Over the years some five thousand Mercers of all sorts were built. Some one hundred or so — a surprisingly small number — still exist. Of these, fewer than half are Raceabouts, both T-head and L-head.

I'm still kicking myself for making my younger brother get back that $5 deposit he put down on an L-head Mercer back in 1935. Where, I asked him, would he ever dig up the other $45 he'd have to pay when he went to collect the car?

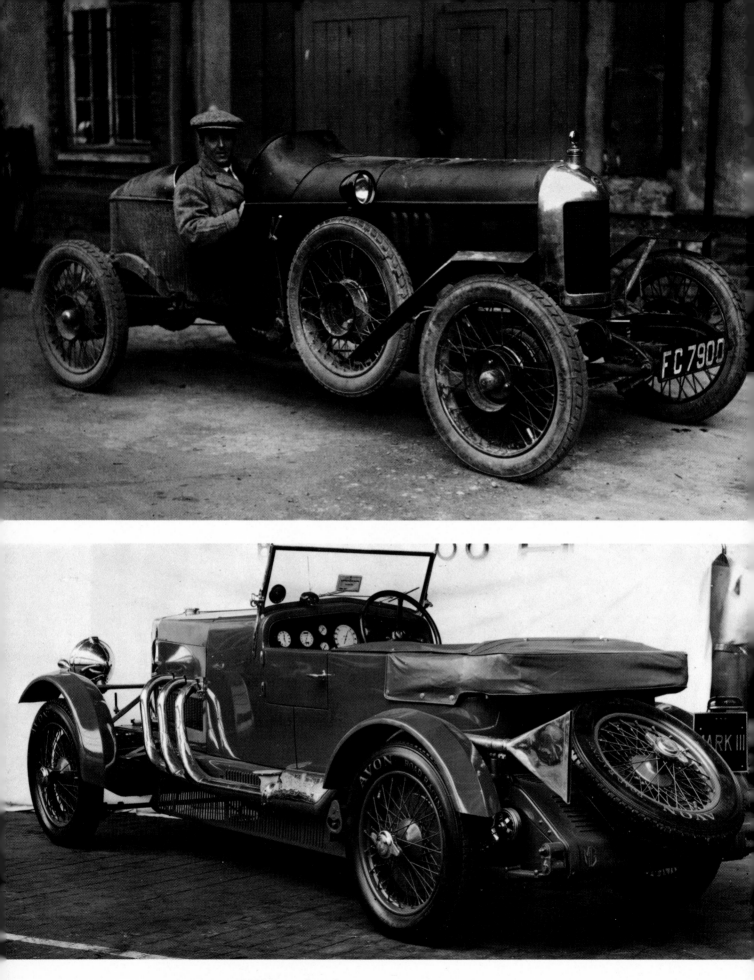

PRECEDING PAGES: 1933 J4 *supercharged*
750-cc road-racing M.G., capable of 110 mph. TOP: *First*
M.G. sports car, Old Number One of 1925,
Cecil Kimber in cockpit. BOTTOM: *2½-litre six-*
cylinder 1930 Mark III Tigress.

M.G. I was, in my youth, a snob about automobiles. In the thirties I looked upon any car but a Bugatti, an Alfa Romeo, or perhaps a Hispano-Suiza, as just not worthy of notice.

"Why," I asked myself, "should I buy a cheap new sports car—an M.G. Midget, a Singer, or even an Amilcar—when for a third of the price, say, $500, I could buy a used Bugatti or an Alfa?" Looking back, I must admit that this disdainful attitude was at least partly wrong. But only partly. Much of the joy of owning a motorcar is in relishing the ingenuities of its construction, the beauties of each lovingly finished surface and curve, the gleam of brass and engine-turned aluminum.

But I might have been better off with a brand-new M.G. Midget, even though it cost more and had a lot less go than a used Bugatti. I'd have had more driving and less tinkering, less paying out of valuable depression-time dollars to mechanics. For it must be admitted now, which I wouldn't do then, that those Bugattis and Alfas were not quite *au point* when I happily drove them home.

The first M.G.'s I saw, in about 1934—except for pictures of them in the English *Autocar* and *Motor*—were J2 types in the hands of the Collier brothers, Miles and Sam. These young men, and sometimes their brother Barron, Jr., already were engaging in the kind of amateur sports-car racing that a later generation of Americans wouldn't discover for fifteen years. They and their friends raced not only M.G.'s, but a long-tailed Brooklands Riley, plus various Amilcars, and a Bugatti or two on their father's estate at Briarcliff Manor, New York, and later through the streets of Alexandria Bay, New York. They had a wonderful time.

The J2 M.G.'s were not-too-distant descendants of the first M-type Midgets of 1929. The M's were not by any means the first M.G.'s, the prototype of which had been built in 1924 or so from Bullnose Morris components at Morris Garages (hence M.G.) by an inspired enthusiast and ex-motorcycle-racer, Cecil Kimber. But the M was the first of the tiny M.G. Midgets. If not for the Midget, the M.G. would most likely have remained merely a very pleasant, medium-sized sporting equipage of so-so quality. I must, however, emphasize that some special M.G.'s, especially those built for racing (the K3 Magnette, for instance), were very fine, very potent mechanisms.

The M, too, was based on a Morris. After all, Kimber and Morris Garages were part of the complex of William Morris (later Lord Nuffield) companies. They had the same four-cylinder, 847-cc, single-overhead-camshaft engines as the Morris Minors, although with more efficient manifolds, and also suffered a fault inherited from the Minor. The camshaft was driven from the crankshaft by a vertically mounted generator, an economy which plagued M.G. owners for years, until the pushrod TA appeared, since oil from the camshaft too often found its way into the electrics.

But the M was a sudden smashing success. It was cheap; in England it cost the equivalent of $800. Its two-seated, pointed-tail, plywood-and-fabric body tickled youthful sports-car types, and its performance, although its engine developed only 20 hp at 4000, wasn't too bad. It would exceed 65 mph, thanks to its 1,250-pound weight. Its competition successes helped, too. In 1930 five M types ran in the Double Twelve, that odd race at Brooklands Track, which was run in two daylight bites of twelve hours each, and all five finished. One of them

OPPOSITE PAGE: 1930
*M type was first
M.G. Midget in production.
It had fabric-and-
wood body, 847-cc four-
cylinder 20-hp
overhead-camshaft engine,
weighed 1,200 pounds.*
RIGHT: *Gaggle of
M.G. Midgets leaves the
Abingdon factory
for delivery.*

ABOVE LEFT: *W. Montgomery
in his M-type Midget
is off for the Monte Carlo
Rally. Note
Marchal headlights.*
ABOVE RIGHT: *C-type
Montlhéry Midgets being
prepared for
1931 Double Twelve race.*
RIGHT: *Team of
J2 Midgets for 1932
London-Edinburgh Trial.*

188

1932-33 750-cc four-
cylinder overhead-camshaft J2
M.G., the archetype Midget.
Its slab tank,
fold-flat windshield,
door cutaways
set M.G. style for the
next twenty years.

Rear aspect of a J2
Midget shows octagon
instruments, a shape which
still means M.G.
Cycle mudguards, which looked
stark and sporting, soon
gave way to sweeping
fenders-cum-running boards.

1936 TA M.G. Midget
no longer had overhead-
camshaft. 1292-cc pushrod
engine outraged purists.
This one, sans headlights, is
undergoing test drive
which all Midgets of that time
had before delivery.

averaged 60.23 mph and came in fourteenth.

But it was a special sports-racing version of the M type from which sprang the unique small sports car that we think of when we say M.G. This was the Montlhéry Midget, the C type, which in order to fit into the international 750-cc racing class had its engine size reduced to 747 cc's. The Montlhéry Midget had an improved chassis, heftier engine bearings, a balanced crankshaft, and in standard form it developed 30 hp. With a 9-to-1 compression ratio for racing, the engine put out 45 hp. The supercharged MKII Montlhérys got up to 60 hp at 6300 rpm. Their success was phenomenal. At the 1931 Double Twelve, Montlhéry Midgets took the first five places and the team prize; in the Irish Grand Prix that same year they were first, third, and fourth.

Based on this wondrous Midget, there appeared in 1932 the lovely-looking little J2 (J1 was an open four-seater, J's 3 and 4 were blown 750's for racing). The J2 was the archetype of all those exactly right looking M.G.'s with which drivers stayed in love for twenty-three long years, until the demise of the TF in 1955. It was low. It was cut crisply sharp. Its doors were notched for its occupants' arms. It had a no-nonsense slab tank slung to its tightly functional stern. Its windshield, forward of a pair of bosom-like windbreakers, folded forward. Above all, it looked as if it meant business and hadn't been diddled with by a lot of mindless "stylists." (Most "stylists" ought to stick to designing purple bathroom conveniences for split-level houses, not motorcars.)

The J2's still used the 847-cc, overhead-cam engine, but now it developed 33 hp at 5000 rpm. Delighted owners playing racer in its lower gears sometimes over-revved the poor little thing, however, and broke its two-bearing crankshaft. Further, its hockey-puck-diameter brakes (8 inches) were discouragingly feeble.

Kimber outfoxed these heavy-footed gentry and in 1934 brought out a new model, the PA, with a slightly longer chassis, a slightly more robust three-bearing crank, and better brakes. Although its 847-cc engine now put out 35 bhp, its power lagged behind the increasing weight of the car (1,600 pounds). So, to get a few more horses, the cylinders were bored out from 57 to 60 millimeters and the PA became the PB.

Altogether, these J's and P's did beautifully in the peculiarly horrifying type of "trials" which the hardy British love: climbing unclimbable, muddy, rock-strewn precipices on rainy midnights. You could, in those happy days, buy real racing M.G.'s directly from the factory. One of these, the nonpareil of all Midgets, before or since, was the blown 750-cc Q type, which put out no less than 113 bhp at 7200 rpm. The Q broke records all over the place—for example, the standing-start mile at 85.59 mph. Trying to outdo themselves, the factory then went all modern and built the R, a single-seater with a design well ahead of its time. This had a backbone chassis strikingly similar to that of the current Lotus Elan, with independent suspension all around. The R showed great promise, but just as its bugs were being eliminated, the M.G. Car Company, which had operated as one of Lord Nuffield's separate entities, became part of Morris Motors Limited, a staid outfit which at that time frowned upon racing. The R died.

It wasn't until 1936 or so that I actually drove an M.G. This was a TA type, and Miles Collier let me take one out, under his watchful eye, in New York's Central Park.

LEFT: 1934 1100-cc
supercharged K3 Magnette.
The Magnette was a
bigger six-cylinder brother
of the Midget,
and the K3 was its racing
version. Nuvolari
drove a K3 to victory in
the 1933 Ulster T.T.

RIGHT: M.G. evolution.
Post-World War II TC
Midget introduced the sports
car to America. By
1949 it had become the
fatter TD, and by
1953 finally metamorphosed
into the still more
obese TF. The TF was the
last Midget to retain
separate fenders, running
boards, and slab tank.

The cops in those days were rather lenient with the few exuberant sports-car drivers who used the park's twisting roads as a test track. (We once even tried to put on a road race there, but they nixed that.)

The TA, in 1936, caused even more heart-burning than the demise of the TC's and TF's a decade later. "Pushrods!" we wailed. "The M.G. is finished without an overhead cam!"

Sadly, the PB's overhead cam *was* gone. The new 1272-cc engine did look like something out of a Chevrolet.

I remember that ride with Collier very well. He took every corner at the limit, his left hand was a blur as he continually changed gear, while double clutching and winding the engine to its screaming limit.

I was impressed. The noise, the wind (the windshield, naturally, was folded flat), Collier's intensity were all most exciting.

When my turn came and I settled myself behind the wheel, everything felt just right: the seat, the wheel position, the fly-off hand brake, the gear-lever placement. Perfect. A lot better than my 1750-cc Alfa.

The car steered almost as well as the Alfa, cornering was flat and accurate. But there was one trouble. The damn thing wouldn't go. It was sluggish, gutless.

Why, then, do I consider the M.G. a "great car"? Was the TB, which superseded the TA, any better? No. Its chief difference was its slightly smaller engine size—1250 cc. Nor was the TC, which appeared after the war, any bomb.

The reason for considering the M.G.—especially the T.C.—"great" is because it changed the American world of automobilism and is still changing it. How did it happen? And why?

The immediate postwar generation of Americans didn't know that such a delightful thing as a sports car even existed. True, their fathers had vague memories of Mercer Race-abouts and Stutz Bearcats. But such machines had long ceased to be available. They were part of an almost mythical past.

Some say that American G.I.'s in England were the ones who first saw the stunning-looking M.G. on its native heath and immediately wanted it. Perhaps that did start things. However, no sooner did the Collier brothers start importing a few—still with right-hand drive and, in the English fashion, bumperless (Zumbach's in New York did a brisk trade making bumpers)—than the rush was on.

Americans were entranced by the TC's clean spiky look, its high thin fenders over tall spidery center-lock wire wheels, the sharp bark from its exhaust, and its fairly low price—about $1,600.

The M.G. was a revelation to thousands of Americans inured to the concoctions of Detroit, which year by year had grown even softer, less maneuverable, more vulgarly embellished by tasteless "stylists" bowing to even more tasteless sales managers. Above all, you could actually see out of an M.G. By 1947 or so, the windows on Detroit's appliances had become mere slits with their lower edges not much above eye level.

But mostly it was the way M.G.'s handled that excited their new owners. Here was a car that went where you pointed it, that didn't roll sickeningly at every bend. The driver was the boss, not the car. And, of course, drivers enjoyed cutting a dashing figure in front of their stodgier neighbors in Hudsons, or the like.

Since M.G.'s *looked* racy and could go around corners fairly rapidly without upsetting, their owners almost immediately

Current MGB *has a four-cylinder 1798-cc pushrod engine of 98 bhp, and a unitized body-cum-chassis. Its 0-to-60 time is about 10.5 seconds. Its claimed top speed: 107 mph. Car has disc brakes.*

joined sports-car clubs and went racing. Looking back, those early races through the streets of Watkins Glen and Bridgehampton dominated, at least in numbers, by M.G.'s seem to have been much more fun than the desperate professional contests of today.

Led by the M.G., other sporting machinery was imported—Jaguar, Aston Martin, Porsche, Triumph. Names unknown before the war became commonplace. Words like "cornering," "roadholding" were bandied about. It took years, but even the nabobs in the fastnesses of Detroit began to hear that many Americans wanted simpler, better-handling motorcars. Very gradually, after almost twenty years, we're beginning to get them, almost.

It was inevitable that after the M.G.'s thumping success the base of ownership would broaden, that many thousands of people who had no interest in the sporting aspects of motoring would buy M.G.'s because they were handy or cute or dashing-looking. These people kicked about the M.G.'s starkness, its hard ride. The next M.G.—the 1949 TD—pleased them but outraged the true believers, for the TD was fatter-looking, had disc wheels, an independent front suspension, and, for export to the U.S., left-hand drive. Now the days of the starkly lovable T series were numbered. In 1952 Syd Enever, M.G.'s designer, had already designed a lower, wider-chassised car with a smooth envelope body. But he had to wait a year for there were big things stir-ring. Nuffield's was about to merge with Austin to form the British Motors Corporation. Also, at this time, the birth pangs of the new Austin Healey were putting the older child, M.G., a bit into the shade.

In 1953, then, the MGA arrived, now no longer a midget. It was bigger and heavier, and had the 1489-cc engine which was also used in some other cars of the Corporation's range. Although the diehards grieved again at its un-M.G.-like shape, the MGA sold wonderfully—over 100,000 in the seven years of its life. Toward the end its engine size was increased to 1622 cc. For a while, too, it was possible to buy an MGA with a twin-overhead-camshaft engine that revved like mad—too madly, perhaps, for exuberant owners who didn't keep one eye on the rev-counter. Fed up with blown-up engines, B.M.C. withdrew it after a couple of years. Meanwhile, a new car was blessed with the magic name—M.G. Midget. But this was merely the tiny Austin Healey Sprite with an M.G.-shaped radiator shell and a new label.

Today the M.G. sports car is the excellent MGB, of which more are sold than any other sports car anywhere. If its slightly stodgy body lines depress you, don't blame its shape on Syd Enever. In his shop at the still bucolic M.G. works at Abingdon, I saw the truly lovely machine he wanted to build. But M.G.'s are big business now and the smart businessmen in charge aren't about to take risks with anything too far out.

Neither would I in their boots.

Jaguar

Jaguar I long considered the Jaguar and its immediate ancestor, the S.S., a parvenu's car, a spurious machine that was all show and no go, whose svelte skin concealed dross beneath. Today my hackles no longer rise (just what is a hackle?) at mention of the name Jaguar. But when a gentleman I knew proposed opening a plush emporium for the sale of foreign cars in the late forties, a time when such machinery was relatively unknown in this country, and asked me which European cars he should handle, I gave him a list of the ones I thought suitable. It included Alfa Romeo, Aston Martin, Bugatti (we still thought Bugattis would again be produced), Delahaye, and some others I can't now recall. But I do remember uttering a dire warning. "Don't let a Jaguar into your showroom," I said. "It will cheapen your whole operation." Luckily for him he paid no attention to my diatribe, and proceeded to acquire a Jaguar agency. The Jaguars outsold every car in the shop and made the man a millionaire.

That conversation took place almost twenty years ago. I have since then made an about-face. I consider the Jaguars of today, especially the most desirable XK-E, among the best cars in the world. There are few cars that can touch an XK-E for sheer looks. It makes even some Ferraris look downright stolid. Its long, long hood, which rises slightly in a sensual curve between its root at the windshield and the purposeful sea-monster mouth, which seems to be sucking air even when the car is standing idle, its high and jaunty derriere, which subtly echoes and supplements the sweep of the hood, the big, no-nonsense wheels, and the reptilian squatness of the entire machine make it a breathtaking exercise in metal sculpture. Most sculptures don't go, but the XK-E

most certainly does, as I found out while co-driving on a longish trip last year. The 4.2 XK-E, unless you drive one daily and remember the drill, isn't the easiest of cars in which to insert yourself. But once I got aboard and behind the wood-rimmed steering wheel, I felt quite comfortably at home, although I could have used another inch or so of leg room. The engine started with that immediate burst of sound somehow characteristic of overhead camshafts.

The short gear lever was in almost the exactly right position and could be flicked from notch to notch without overriding the synchromesh. (The 4.2 has a far better gearbox than the 3.8 XK-E.) The clutch was soft and silky. The only thing that really bothered me was that sexy hood. It dropped off ahead, I knew not where; I had to learn that the front end of the car was a foot or so farther forward than it looked to be.

But after a short time on the road, these carping little points seemed unimportant. The car performed beautifully, brilliantly, and in gentlemanly fashion. You might think that a machine easily capable of 150 mph, and 0 to 60 in well under 7 seconds, would at some point bare its teeth and become a wild beast, but not the Jaguar. Of course, we never did get up to 150; you just can't between Connecticut and Cape Cod. But we often, momentarily, touched 110 and leaving toll booths we once or twice accelerated through the gears as hard as possible — no sweat, no funny sounds from the engine room, no smell of cooking from the clutch, and no overheating in spite of the 90-degree weather. On our return trip we took the Jaguar home over the narrow, many-cornered back roads of Connecticut. There the car's impeccable steering really shone. Perhaps we didn't try hard enough, but its

198

PRECEDING PAGES: 1937 SS-100 *looks more like a sports car than almost any machine ever built. "100" in name denotes top speed, but only a brave man would — considering its less-than-perfect roadholding — try to drive it that fast.*

TOP: *Jaguar company (then known as Swallow)*
was in body-building business before producing cars.
This is Swallow-bodied Austin Seven.
BOTTOM: *SS-I of 1933 had rakish coachwork, looked*
quick, but wouldn't do much over 70 mph.

ABOVE: *Duncan
Hamilton in D-type Jaguar
negotiating David's
Hairpin at Brands Hatch,
England, in 1957.
Note typical D-type fin.*

RIGHT: *XK-120 was,
in 1950, first of postwar
sporting Jaguars.
This is model that made
marque the pet of
sports drivers in U.S.*

ABOVE: *Sports Jaguars were raced with enthusiasm by American drivers. This starting lineup is for Fort Worth-Eagle Mt. race in Texas.*

LEFT: *C-type Jaguar became famous for its 1951 victory in Le Mans 24-hour race. Peter Walker and Peter Whitehead shared driving.*

tail stuck like epoxy—it never did break away. And no matter how hard we braked, the disc brakes never faded.

The XK-E has what is by now an almost venerable engine, basically that which first powered the XK-120 of almost twenty years ago. But where that old XK-120 had but 160 hp (and we thought that phenomenal), the XK-E 4.2 engine puts out a hefty 265 hp. Of course, the engine has changed greatly over the years. The bores are bigger and differently spaced, which has meant new block castings, and the crankshaft has been redesigned for increased stiffness. And there are three S.U. carburetors compared to two in that original 3.4-litre engine of 1948. Strangely, however, the long stroke is still traditionally English (3.625-inch bore, 4.17-mm stroke), which seems slightly archaic in a day of over-square engines and tends to limit engine revs.

There are only three cars which can challenge the XK-E 4.2 in its class: the Ferrari, Aston Martin, and Corvette. Compared to Ferrari and Aston at around $15,000, the Jaguar is a surprising bargain at about $6,000. The Corvette is roughly in the same price class, but both the Corvette and the XK-E 4.2 are semi-mass-produced articles and you must expect small deficiencies.

William Lyons (now Sir William) started building cars inside-out. Most people who go into the automobile business first build chassis and then look around for some means of clothing them. But Lyons was in the body-building business first and he even got into that in an unusual manner. First, in the English beach resort of Blackpool, in 1922, he and a partner started building bright aluminum sidecars for motorcycles. They were exactly what young Britons of the motorcycle set were looking for. And the

imposingly named "Swallow Side Car and Coach Building Company" prospered.

In the mid-twenties, Swallow branched out and began doing for the dull little mass-produced British cars what it had done for the homely sidecar. It gave them what Detroit now calls "pizzaz." Swallow bedizened prosaic little Austins, Wolseleys, Swifts, and Standards with curvaceous, revoltingly colored coachwork.

The successful Lyons next arranged with the Standard Motor Company to supply him with elongated, double-dropped frames, complete with other chassis components— engine, transmission, brakes, etc.—upon which he could start building a car of his own. He named his new car the S.S. for Standard Swallow or, as some now claim, Swallow Sports.

The S.S. was first shown at the 1931 London Show. It was the kind of car romantic errand boys dream about, all hood and no passenger compartment. Sadly, however, the S.S. cars (there were two models, the SS-I and the SS-II) were not really terribly sporting. The SS-I could be ordered with either a 2-litre or a 2½-litre, L-head engine. The larger engine produced 48 hp and a top speed of about 70 mph. You can imagine the verve of the 1-litre-engined SS-II. These early SS's sold amazingly well, however, and SS-I cost only $1,500.

Lyons didn't remain shackled to those gutless Standard engines for long. He had a new and excellent 2½-litre pushrod ohv engine designed, and started building a line of much improved machines, both sedans and open sports cars. Among these were two sports cars which are still much desired today: the SS-90 and the SS-100 (the numbers designated their top speeds). The SS-90 was built before the new ohv engine was ready, but the SS-100 (now with the name Jaguar added) had the new power plant, at first in 2½-litre form, later in 3½ litre. Both would reach their claimed speeds and both were wonderful buys even in the late thirties. The 3½ litre cost only $2,175. For his money, the sports-car enthusiast got a car that was and still is the archetype of what such a machine should look like. With its long, louvered hood, bucket seats well aft, swooping fenders, goggling P-100's, it was enough to make a fellow swoon. And it went, too. Zero to 60 in 11 seconds. But only a hero would avail himself of an SS-100's top speed. I remember trying it once and frightening myself silly when the beast started dancing about at anything over 80.

The Mark IV was the first postwar Jaguar. By then the initials SS had disappeared. The Mark IV was little changed from the 3½-litre 1939 Jaguar, but sold like mad to Americans for almost $5,000. People liked its woodwork, its leather, its quicker-than-American steering. But it rode a mite hard for Americans used to the bed-like softness of Detroit cars, and in 1948 was superseded by the independently sprung Mark V.

The Mark IV and Mark V were still descendants of the SS. But in 1948 Jaguar started down another path with an entirely new concept in cars: the XK-120, which is the true precursor of today's line of Jaguar cars. With its 3.4-litre overhead-camshaft engine and short, 104-inch wheelbase, the radical new machine took America, which had just discovered the sports car (mostly the TC M.G.) by storm. In 1950, the first year you could buy one, over five thousand XK-120's were sold. Another five thousand were snapped up the following year. The XK hadn't been designed for racing. In fact, its engine had been originally meant for a sedan, but private owners immediately ripped off their windshields, taped over their lights, and started racing. Soon Jaguar factory teams began cleaning up all over the place, and a try at the hour record was made at Jabbeke in Belgium. They managed to put 132.6 miles into the hour, but Bugatti's record of 135.4 miles, made ten years earlier in a stock 57S, still stood.

The XK-120 became more powerful (and fatter) year after year: 190 hp in the XK-140, 265 hp in the XK-150S. Sedans—the bulbous Mark 7 and its later versions, the 3.4, the 2.4, and the Mark 10—all used variations of the same engine.

In 1951, the factory built a racing sports car, the envelope-bodied C-type with which it won at Le Mans. In 1954 the D-type sports-racing Jaguar had the monocoque, chassis-less construction which was later to appear in the XK-E. But first this engineering showed up in the aborted, but delectable XK-SS, first seen in 1957. Only sixteen of these fine machines, which were practically D-types with windshields and bumpers, were finished before the factory burned and stopped production.

When rebuilt, the factory went on to the more sophisticated, independently sprung all around, disc-braked E-type—the XK-E. And the current line of sedans, the 340 and the 420, with that same puissant overhead-camshaft engine, full independent suspension, and disc brakes, still carry on William Lyons' tradition of the most for the least money.

British Motors Corporation have recently bought the Jaguar empire, which by now includes Daimler, Guy (the truck and bus builders), and Coventry Climax, who latterly have been famous for racing engines.

I wonder what the B.M.C.'s XK-F will be like.

ABOVE LEFT: *XK-SS was precursor of current XK-E. Sixteen were built in 1957 before a fire ended production.*

LEFT: *2+2 4.2-litre XK-E, stretched version of XK-E two-seater, provides room for four, is 10 inches longer.*

TOP RIGHT: *1957 XK-150 was faster, bulkier than XK-120. 150S form had 265 hp compared to 160 hp of XK-120.*

CENTER RIGHT: *Current Jaguar 420G Grand Saloon has same six-cylinder overhead-camshaft engine as the XK-E.*

BOTTOM RIGHT: *3.8-litre Mark II at 1963 German Nürburgring. Peter Lindner drove it to third successive victory there.*

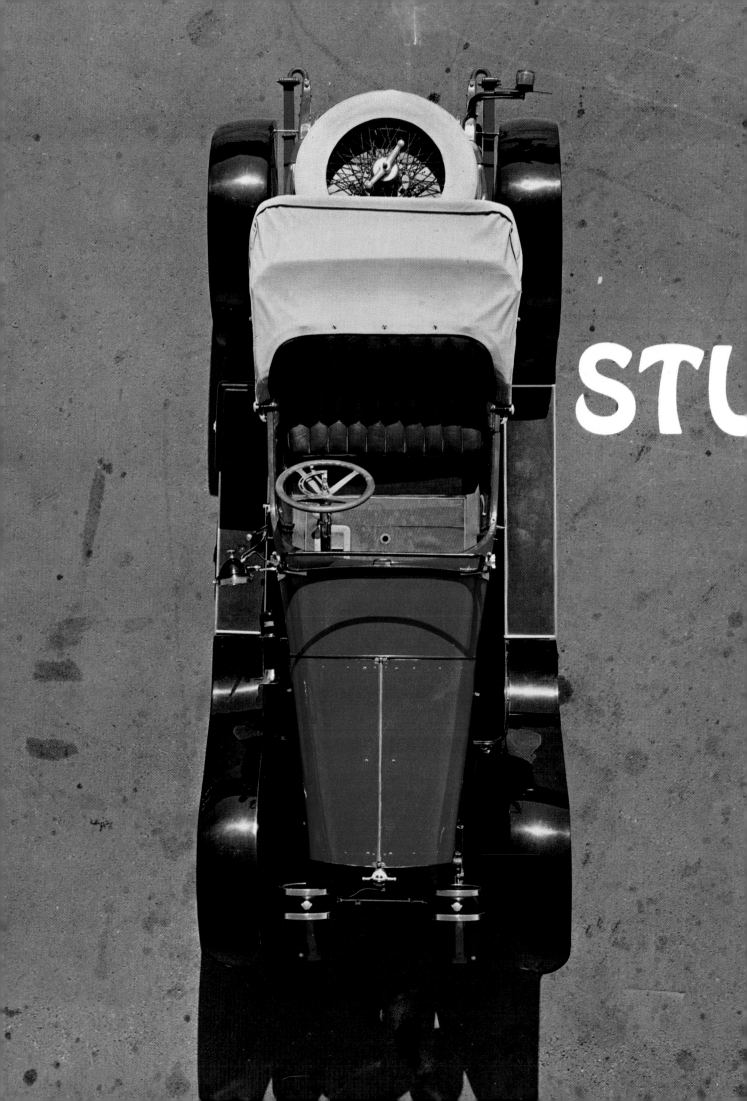

STU

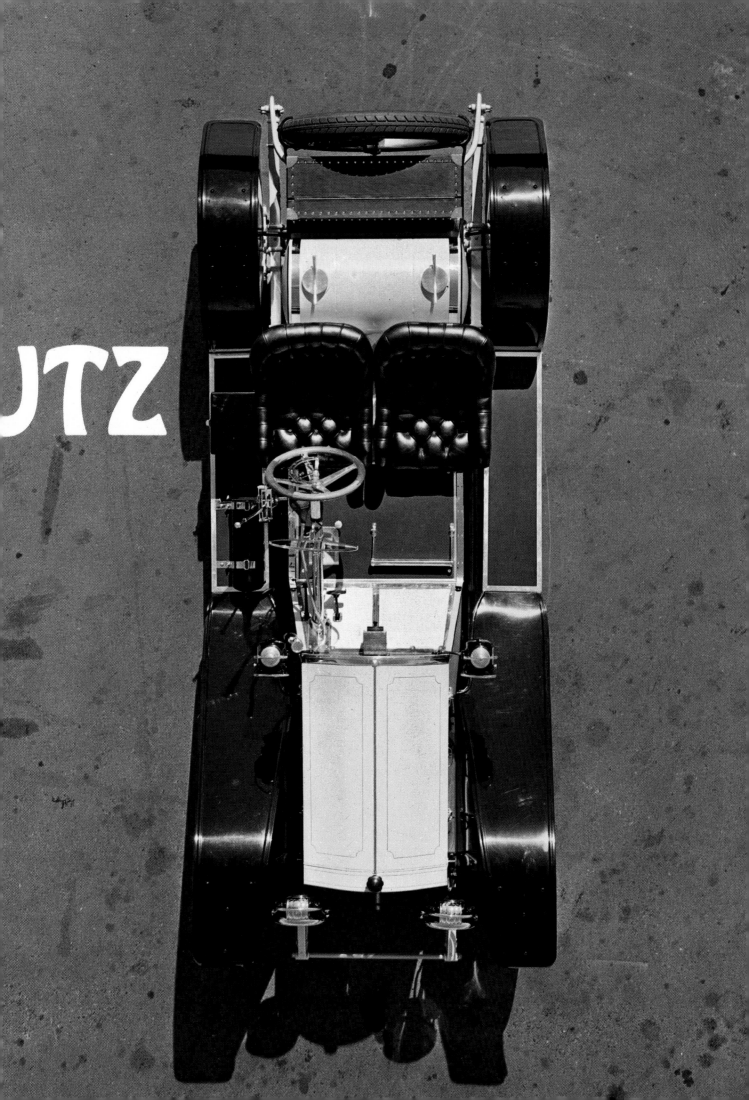

JTZ

STUTZ The Stutz, like Paul Bunyan or the Twentieth Century Limited, is part of America's folklore. Mention the name "Stutz Bearcat" and you instantly evoke visions of flappers in cloche hats and 1920's-style miniskirts, of "cake-eater" suits and raccoon coats and hip flasks.

This anachronism, and it seems to be an anachronism because the time of the open, bucket-seat Bearcat was over by 1920, has bothered me for a long time. Why should a car of World War I days be so resolutely considered a glamorous part of the dizzy twenties? What could be the truth only recently dawned upon me. It's simply this. The youths of the twenties must have bought used Bearcats, Mercers, and Marmons. They couldn't have bought new ones because such cars were not only disappearing but cost too much.

I didn't ride in a Bearcat until 1935 or so. I had remembered a very red Bearcat, one of the later ones with proper doors and a spare tire sunk into a well on its afterdeck. But I had only seen it from a distance, for it was always parked in the driveway of a slightly disheveled old mansion whose blinds were drawn in the daytime and from which sounds of ragtime piano playing came at all hours. I was not permitted to enter its yard for a closer inspection of the Bearcat.

The Bearcat in which I traveled years afterward was owned by Smith Hempstone Oliver, who later became Curator of Land Transportation at the Smithsonian Institution. In those days venerable motorcars (and the Stutz, at age twenty-one, wasn't all that venerable) weren't nurtured and coddled as are early cars today and Oliver used his as ordinary transport in New York.

I owned a 1750 cc Alfa at the time and I was used to its lowness and the feeling of

being part of the car which it gave me. Just sitting way up high in the Stutz, in a tiny bucket seat on an open platform with a doghouse hood out front and a drum-shaped gas tank behind, made me uncomfortable. When Oliver took off with a crunch of gears and a bound as he let in the clutch, I was nervous. When he started swooping in and out of New York's antic traffic and admitted to having only rudimentary brakes, I was downright scared. But that big, bellowing lump of a car would go. Oliver not only kept up with the fast-moving Manhattan traffic, he managed to leave most of the stop-light Grand Prix types behind, too. I must admit that that first ride in that ungainly Stutz permanently infected me with a desire for such brutish old motorcars.

The 1914 Bearcat was the first of Harry C. Stutz's cars to have that ursine label. But Stutz had built cars before that. He had built a crude gas buggy in 1897, when he was only twenty. By 1905 he was building the American Underslung, that radical, low-center-of-gravity machine whose chassis was hung below its springs and axles.

Stutz first made his name famous by building a car to demonstrate the sturdiness of the rear axles produced by his Stutz Motor Parts Company. He then entered this machine in the first Indianapolis "500" in 1911 and came in eleventh. The car had run faultlessly and Stutz put similar machines into production with the slogan "The Car That Made Good In A Day."

Stutz didn't make his own components in those days. He bought parts and like many another maker turned out what was called an "assembled car." He used Wisconsin T-head engines at first, but by 1913 he was building his own four- and six-cylinder power plants. His cars were again success-

208

PRECEDING PAGES: 1920 *Bearcat (left) and 1912 Bearcat (right) show civilizing effects of eight years: top, windshield, and doors have been added. Collectors today would opt for older model.*

1933 *Stutz Super Bearcat. This was last of the sporting Stutz's before factory ceased production. In this side view it looks impossibly short and stubby, but actual cars were quite good-looking.*

ful and took a third place at Indianapolis in 1913.

The Bearcat of 1914 (Stutz also produced a less sporting Bulldog) had a 6½-litre, four-cylinder, T-head engine which developed 60 hp at 1500 rpm. Its three-speed gearbox and differential were in a single unit in the rear axle.

This was the time of the great Stutz-Mercer rivalry. Stutz owners were supposed to have sung, "There never was a worser car than a Mercer," and Mercer owners, "You have to be nuts to drive a Stutz." Perhaps the "Twenty-three Skidoo" sports of 1914 were that corny, but I doubt it. Anyhow, the Mercer protagonists were indubitably right. The Bearcat was a coarse, rough, high load of iron compared to the far more refined and better-handling Mercer Raceabout. I must admit, however, that the more highly powered Stutz won more races than Mercer. In 1915 Stutz built a special team of racing cars with overhead-camshaft Wisconsin engines. Known as the "White Squadron" (they were painted white and the drivers wore white coveralls), they came in third, fourth, and seventh at Indianapolis and took firsts at Elgin, Minneapolis, and Sheepshead Bay.

There was nothing stodgy about the Stutz Company. It was always willing to take a sporting chance. In 1916, when a disgruntled Bearcat buyer brought his car back to a New York dealer and grumbled that Mercers were passing him even though his car had a bigger engine, they took it back and had it checked by their mechanics. The mechanics said they couldn't find anything wrong.

The sales people then set up a publicity scheme. They advertised that this so-called lemon of a Stutz would be given to "Cannonball" Baker for an attack on the coast-to-coast record then held by, of all things, a motorcycle. The roads across America were almost nonexistent in 1916. West of Omaha the rocky, muddy trail wasn't even signposted. But "Cannonball" beat the record and crossed the country in eleven days, seven and a half hours, faster than anything but a train had ever done it. One day he put in an incredible 592 miles. The car came through almost perfectly, breaking only a shock-absorber clip.

In 1919 Harry C. Stutz quit the company and went off to build a car called the H.C.S. It was not too successful.

Steel-mogul Charles M. Schwab and a group of associates then took over and the company began to drift into the doldrums with the last version of the Bearcat, now with a monoblock Wisconsin engine, a Speedway four, and a six with pushrod-overhead valves.

In 1925 Stutz came to life again with Frederic E. Moscovics as president. Moscovics announced that henceforth the Stutz image would eschew sportiness and speed and would concentrate on "safety, beauty and comfort." To this end the 1926 model was known as the Safety Stutz. Oddly, however, in spite of Moscovics' pronouncements,

TOP, LEFT & RIGHT: *1931 Weymann-bodied Monte Carlo D.V.32 sedan. Stutz was one of few American makers to use Weymann system in which bodies were built of leatherlike fabric on flexibly jointed wooden framework.*

ABOVE, LEFT & RIGHT: *1927 Stutz Black Hawk boat-tail speedster, similar to machines which ran in Le Mans 24-hour race. Engine was overhead-camshaft straight-eight, produced 95 hp. Underslung worm-drive rear axle was unusual.*

the Stutz became a more sporting machine than ever, and some models were for years the only real sports cars produced in this country.

The Safety Stutz was, for its day, a remarkable machine. It had a straight-eight engine of 4.7 litres and a single, chain-driven, overhead camshaft which, like the Hispano-Suiza and the later, prewar Alfa Romeo, had means for valve adjustment without pulling the whole shebang apart (as I must do on my 1962 Alfa). It produced 92 hp at 3200 rpm. The rest of the car was equally advanced. It had a worm-drive rear axle which permitted a really low chassis and excellent road holding. Its brakes, unusual for its time, were hydraulic by means of water- and alcohol-filled bags which pressed six brake shoes against each brake drum. In sedan form it could better 75 mph.

Happily, Stutz didn't build only sedans; it also produced the wonderful, two-seater Black Hawk based on the same chassis. This name came from racing-genius Frank Lockhart's 3-litre, Miller-engined, land speed-record car which Stutz built. Lockhart was killed in it at Daytona, but earlier he had set the still-amazing, American Class D record at 198.29 mph.

By 1928 the Black Hawk speedster could develop some 125 hp and it was one of those that got into that peculiar race against the Boulogne Hispano-Suiza (see page 48) which had almost twice its power.

It was a Stutz Black Hawk which so shook the "Bentley Boys" at Le Mans in 1928 by very nearly winning from three 4½-litre Bentleys. It lost top gear at 2:30 p.m., but it still took second place behind Barnato, the best showing an American car ever made at Le Mans until the Fords' big victory in 1966.

W. O. Bentley later said in his autobiography, "The Stutz was particularly formidable with its lower frame and superior cornering to the Bentley..."

In 1929 Stutz tried again at Le Mans but did no better than fifth place.

Meanwhile, the Black Hawk was being continually improved. By 1930 almost 100 mph was possible from the now larger 5¼-litre engine. Brakes were better, too, the company having switched to Lockheed hydraulics, and a four-speed gearbox was standard. It was even theoretically possible to buy a supercharged Stutz. Twenty-four of them had been built to meet the Le Mans rules about catalogue models. They had their blowers out front à la Bentley 4½, but I've never seen one, nor has anyone else I know.

In 1930 it became obvious that the Stutz needed more power to counter the big twelve- and sixteen-cylindered Packards, Lincolns, and Cadillacs. The Stutz Company was not healthy enough to go for an entirely new engine in that depression year.

Since the block and crankshaft were capable of delivering many more horsepower, a new cylinder head with twin-overhead camshafts was put into production. This was the famous D.V. 32, with four valves per cylinder. The car was now known as the D.V. 32 Stutz and came in many models. Now, too, the name "Bearcat" was reborn in the Bearcat Torpedo Speedster and the Super Bearcat, a chunky, bobtailed convertible.

The Super Bearcat was Stutz' swan song. By 1935 Stutz was no longer building cars. The company tried to keep afloat for a while by making a thing called a Pak-Age-Car, but even that was ahead of its time.

There wasn't to be a real sports car built in America until the Corvette some twenty years later.

211

Delage

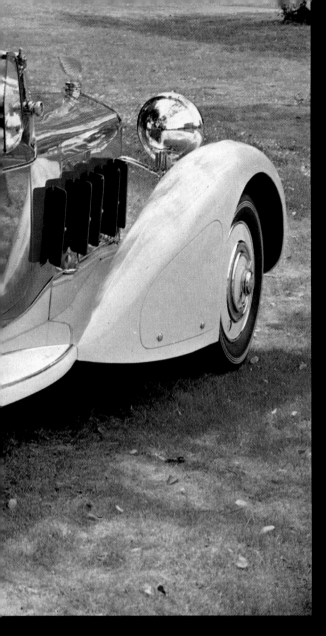

PRECEDING PAGES:
1931 D8S *Delage with Mlle. Renée Friderich at wheel during a Paris-St. Raphael Rally. Delages were darlings of great French coachbuilders—Saoutchik, Letournier et Marchand, Chapron all built elegant bodies for them.*

ABOVE RIGHT: *Lalique hood ornament of type that adorned fancy French cars.*
ABOVE LEFT: *1932 D8S belonging to restaurateur André Surmain.*

LEFT & RIGHT: *Closed and open versions of D8/120.*

Delage

The Delage was *the* car of the *jeunesse dorée* of the thirties, at least of those for whom a Type 57 Bugatti was just too mechanical. It certainly was not the poor man's Hispano-Suiza, for a Delage cost quite as much as one of the six-cylinder pushrod Hispanos—circa $5,000—rather more than a bourgeois might spend for a car. (As for the big twelve-cylinder Hispano-Suiza, it was not a car for the mere millionaire; at around $20,000, it was only for billionaires—in francs, naturally.)

A particular Delage with which I became fairly well acquainted was the quite luxurious D8/120 machine owned by collector Robert S. Grier. This beautifully bodied convertible by Letournier et Marchand was, alongside various Bugattis and a Delahaye or two, one of the proudly exhibited productions of the French motor industry at the 1939 New York World's Fair. No sooner did Grier see this jewel than he just had to have it. After much complicated maneuvering and haggling with the people in charge, Grier managed to actually buy the car. But when the fair shut down, it was up to him to remove it from the below-ground-level, glass-enclosed rotunda at the base of the French Pavilion.

A series of steps encircled the exhibition area and it was necessary to remove some of the windows and then lay planks on the steps up which the Delage would ostensibly be pushed. I say ostensibly, because Grier had no intention of pushing that 4,000-pound-plus car uphill. He had, however, to pretend that such was his plan since a phalanx of New York City firemen stood by, resolutely determined that no gasoline engine would be started inside that French Pavilion. Werner Maeder of Zumbach's, who had driven out from New York with Grier

and me, was fully equipped to get the Delage started, firemen or no. He installed a freshly charged battery, greased this and oiled that from a selection of oil cans and grease guns and syringes and, while thus engaged, managed to fill the float chambers of the carburetors with fuel. Grier slid behind the wheel appearing to check something for Maeder; I made sure the planks were in place, the windows open. Maeder whispered to Grier. And before you could say knife, the Delage roared up the planks and out into the winter-empty World's Fair and then stalled—out of gas. The firemen, outwitted, pretended to have no further interest in the Delage. Grier added some fuel and we were off.

Grier used the Delage for some ten years and I became quite enamored of it. Although not too quick (it took some 16 seconds to go from 0 to 60), since its eight-cylinder engine only developed about 120 bhp, it held the road beautifully and was, for its day, as useful a road express as you could wish for.

It was superbly comfortable, much more so, for example, than the low-chassis, S type Invicta which I owned at the time. Its transverse leaf-spring independent front suspension, similar to that in some present-day Ford trucks and in pre-1949 Studebakers, helped. But Grier was never quite able to keep up with the Invicta when we were both trying.

This Delage had a four-speed Cotal electric gearbox. You could change gear clutchlessly merely by moving a tiny lever in a miniature gate on the steering column which looked like that on an 810 Cord. But Cotal gear ratios, in which each was twice that of the one above it, didn't provide a close enough ratio between top and third. And, although quite effortless, the system was not

entirely trouble free (Grier was always diddling with wires under the front floor) and
didn't make for a very sporting change-down
for cornering or passing.

Louis Delage had started building cars
in 1906. Based on single-cylinder De Dion
engines, his cars were beautifully constructed
and immediately successful. Beginning with
three employees, he had eighty-five by 1907
and 350 by 1912, in which year he sold one
thousand machines due, at least in part, to
Delage's racing success. His *Coupe de l'Auto
voiturettes* came in first and third at Boulogne in 1911. In 1913 Delage entered several 6¼-litre cars for the French Grand
Prix, but tire trouble prevented a win. However, one of them, driven by René Thomas,
won the Indianapolis "500" in 1914. It is
this car which famed collector Ed Roy
found in bits (and not all the bits, either)
and restored to its present remarkable,
better-than-new condition.

Delage produced many racing machines,
including a 10.7-litre V-12 which succeeded
in taking the land speed record at 143.24
mph in 1923. But it is the 1500-cc Grand

217

RIGHT: *Poster showing René Thomas'
Delage which won 1914 "500" at Indianapolis.*
BELOW: *Chiron in the
1500-cc Grand Prix Delage at Indianapolis.*

BOTTOM LEFT: *Blown 1500-cc engine
of Grand Prix Delage. Originally built for
1926-27 Formula, remarkable eight-cylinder
power plant developed 170 hp at 8000 rpm.*

BOTTOM RIGHT: *Not all Delages had French
coachwork. This English-bodied convertible is
shown at Ramsgate concours d'élègance.
Six-cylinder D6-70 chassis first appeared in 1936.*

Prix car built for the 1926-1927 formula which is perhaps the most fascinating racing car of all time.

Its engine, brilliantly designed by M. Lory, astounds us even today. Supercharged, it had eight small cylinders in line and put out 170 bhp at 8000 rpm. (English race driver Richard Seaman in 1937 rebuilt his to turn out no less than 195 bhp!) The engine had an incredible number of gears and ball and roller bearings. Twenty gears were used to drive the overhead camshafts, the oil pumps, and the magneto. Sixty ball and roller bearings revolved inside the gears, on the nine-main-bearing crankshaft, and on practically every turning surface M. Lory could think of. The twin camshafts alone took eighteen of them.

In the four Grand Prix races which these Delages entered in 1927, they came in first four times. And in two of the races they also took second and third place.

It wasn't until 1925 that the touring Delage became a very interesting machine. The DIS appeared that year and became an even more desirable car—lower and faster and known as the DISS—the following year. The 14-40 DISS had a four-cylinder 2120-cc engine, pushrod overhead valves, and a top speed of 80 mph—fast for 1927. It was well built and had fine road manners. Some British enthusiasts are still enjoying DISS's with hundreds of thousands of miles on their clocks. In fact, so sturdy were these DISS's that three years ago one of them, converted to a tow car, dragged a badly wrecked car in which I was a passenger many miles from a remote French village to a large town where we could get help. The chief flaw of these very nice cars is their less-than-lovable Ducellier dyna-motors—starters-cum-generators.

In 1930 Delage built a straight-eight, the 4-litre D8, which would approach 100 mph. The D8SS, a super-sports short-chassis version of 1932, which developed 120 bhp at 4000 rpm, could easily exceed 100 mph and with slight modification could do rather better, one of these D8SS's averaging 112 mph for twelve hours at the Montlhéry track.

By 1936 the Delage operation was in parlous condition. Somehow Louis Delage had lost interest and let things slide a bit. Delahaye bought out Delage. But Delahaye, unlike many companies which acquire their rivals, continued to build great Delages—for example the very fine D8/120.

The D8/120 was as exciting-looking a machine as anyone could pine for. Outside exhaust pipes and svelte coachwork by such famous automotive couturiers as Figoni and Falaschi, Letournier et Marchand, and Saoutchik made the D8/120 *the* car in front of which many an expensive Folies Bergère blonde posed for *L'Illustration* when her industrialist boy friend entered the car for a *concours d' élègance*.

But the straight-eight cost too much for the tight purses of the thirties and in 1936 the D6-70 was brought out. It was with these 6's that Delage began again to be successful in competition. In 1938, Louis Gerard won the Tourist Trophy in one at Donington Park, England, and came in second at Le Mans behind a 57C Bugatti. In 1949, at the first postbellum Le Mans, Louveau and Jouer took second place to the Chinetti-Selsdon Ferrari, and Delage took the top three places in the 3-litre class.

But Delage—and Delahaye—didn't last much longer. In 1953, the peculiar French income-tax system, which assumes you're very rich if you own a car which cost a lot of francs, did them in.

LINCOLN

CARAVANE AU CANADA FRANÇAIS

13

19   C.C.C.A.   66

LINCOLN The first Lincoln of 1920 was the culmination of the lifelong devotion to precision of that archetype of persnickety Yankee toolmakers, Henry M. Leland. Born in 1843, Leland had learned his craft well. At the Colt Arms Factory he learned what true parts interchangeability meant. At Brown and Sharpe, makers of the world's most accurate micrometers and machine tools, he worked to tolerances of four-millionths of an inch. Later at Leland & Faulconer, his own plant in Detroit, he built auto engines for the Detroit Automobile Company, and when it transformed itself to the Cadillac Automobile Company, he became its head. While at Cadillac, Leland showed the world what he meant by interchangeability of accurately machined parts. In 1908, he took three Cadillacs to England, had them dismantled, jumbled up the parts, and proceeded quickly to reassemble three Cadillacs out of the well-mixed bits.

In 1917, William Crapo Durant, president of General Motors, which by then owned Cadillac, refused to let Leland build Liberty aero engines. Leland, seventy-four years old, quit and took his son Wilfred, who was a top Cadillac executive, with him. He formed the Lincoln Motor Company and built 6,500 Liberty engines by war's end.

The 1920 Lincoln was a mechanical triumph but an esthetic disaster. It had a 5.77-litre, V-8, L-head engine which delivered 90 hp at 2800 rpm. The radiator was built of seamless copper tubing and had thermostatically controlled shutters long before Rolls-Royce adopted them. It was possible to run from 3 to 73 mph in *top* gear. But the bodies Leland mounted on his $4,300-to-$6,000 gems were, if beautifully constructed, nauseating to look at. Many orders were canceled.

Other troubles piled up. In 1921, Lincoln was forced into receivership, and Ford bought the company for $8,000,000, about half what Leland thought it was worth. The Lelands couldn't get along with old Henry and soon walked out. Edsel Ford became president of Lincoln.

But the Fords did not in any way cheapen the Lincoln. They improved it and at the same time reduced its price by $1,000. A new cylinder head was designed and aluminum pistons replaced the early cast-iron ones. Acceleration and speed—85 mph in 1923—improved so that the Lincoln, which could run away and hide from Packards and Cadillacs, became the favorite of bootleggers and cops.

The design of Lincoln coachwork improved out of all recognition. Some of the bodies were by Brunn, others were built in a "custom" shop set up by Lincoln. Later the greatest of American *carrossiers*, Judkins, Dietrich, Locke, Murphy, and the others, supplied custom bodies.

But, except for the introduction of four-wheel brakes in 1927 (seventeen years after Isotta!), it was not until 1931 that any great changes were made in Henry Leland's original design. The new Model K, still using Leland's basic engine, now had 120 hp and a new 145-inch chassis. Bodies were lower, tires fatter, radiator shells more pointed. By now coachwork on Lincolns, especially by the custom builders, was truly beautiful. For the next five years Lincoln bodies reached a peak of visual perfection that has seldom been surpassed by anyone anywhere.

In 1932, in spite of the economic storm, Lincoln outdid itself with a new model, the KB, whose 7½-litre, V-12 engine could push the giant 145-inch-wheelbase beauties at over 100 mph in a cathedral hush, broken only by the swish of tires. In 1933 the old V-8

222

PRECEDING PAGES: 1933 KB *Lincoln with Le Baron convertible body.* RIGHT, ABOVE: *When Ford took over Lincoln in 1922, bodies were redesigned. Note drum headlights and crowned fenders, which first appeared in 1925.* RIGHT: *1934 KB coupe.* FAR RIGHT: *Pleasantly ugly Leland Lincoln of 1921.*

was dropped and a smaller engined KA V-12 (6.3 litres) supplemented the lovely KB.

The standard of perfection at the Lincoln factory is almost unbelievable to us today. Testing was as thorough as that at Rolls-Royce. Cars were shipped in dust-proof paper bags in closed freight cars which were first meticulously cleaned inside.

By 1934 even the mighty Ford empire began to be aware of the depression. Mass-production techniques started to infect Lincoln. From now on an enlarged version

of the V-12 KA engine (now 7 litres) powered both the 136-inch KA chassis and the 145-inch KB chassis. And until the end of the classic Lincoln in 1940, there were few mechanical changes.

The Zephyr of 1936 was not a Lincoln. The Lincoln Continental of 1940 was not quite a Lincoln either. It was based on the Lincoln Zephyr and used its twelve-cylinder enlargement of the Ford V-8 engine. I will, however, admit that the Lincoln Continental was prettier than the Zephyr.

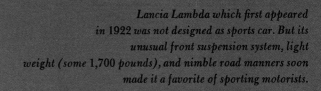

*Lancia Lambda which first appeared
in 1922 was not designed as sports car. But its
unusual front suspension system, light
weight (some 1,700 pounds), and nimble road manners soon
made it a favorite of sporting motorists.*

LANCIA

The Expressway—"the world's longest parking lot"—has obliterated it by now, but some years ago there existed near my home on Long Island an old stone railroad bridge whose single narrow arch spanned a skinny bit of road. Each time I slowly drove under it I was uncomfortably conscious of the too-close proximity of its rough stone piers. But a picture I later saw in an old automobile magazine shamed me. It showed a monstrous F.I.A.T. racing car emerging at speed from under the same structure followed by a great plume of dust which almost obscured the bowler-hatted spectators draped over the bridge. The driver was Vincenzo Lancia, the race was the Vanderbilt Cup of 1905.

Vincenzo was a bulky, mustachioed fellow who favored turtleneck sweaters and was a madman behind the wheel. He had started racing when he was nineteen; he was only twenty-four when he drove in the Vanderbilt. But as usual that day he couldn't resist histrionics and threw away an excellent chance of winning.

Roaring out of his pit after a refueling stop, he neglected to look rearward, shot into the path of a front-drive Christie, injuring the Christie's riding mechanic and making matchwood of the F.I.A.T.'s rear wheels. Still, he managed to finish fourth.

In spite of such shenanigans, Lancia is still remembered as one of the great drivers of his time who helped reap kudos for the name of F.I.A.T. But Vincenzo must have tired of making F.I.A.T. great, for in 1907 he started to build cars under his own name.

The early Lancias with four-cylinder, L-head engines were quite conventional machines noted mostly for their excellent workmanship. Still, they were not entirely stodgy. One of them managed to win the Automobile Club of America's "International Light Car Race" in Savannah, Georgia, in 1908. Lancia used Greek letters in naming his cars. Starting with Alfa (the Italian form of alpha and no connection with Alfa Romeo), he proceeded through Dialfa (a six), Beta, Gamma, Delta, etc.

But if none of these machines was particularly exciting, the Lambda, the wonderful car Vincenzo Lancia brought out in 1922, forever placed the name among the *Grand Marques*. The Lambda was not conceived as a sports car. In Lancia's eyes it was a light tourer. But it was so exactly right, and such a delight to drive as fast as it would go (70 in early models, 85 or so later on) that it has made a place for itself among the most endearing sports cars ever built.

The Lambda had a look all its own. It was unbelievably long (135-inch wheelbase), and although high off the ground it was still a low car because it was such a thin, flat slab of an automobile, like a plank on tall, skinny wheels. At its distant stern was a curiously shaped, hump-like protuberance—the trunk, which had about enough room for an extra pair of driving gloves. The passengers stuck way up out of the body and the windshield was, of necessity, tall. The painted radiator shell was shaped like that of a Rolls-Royce but with the corners rounded off. Sounds terrible! But it was clean, businesslike, and pleasingly unconventional.

The Lambda was one of the first cars (after the Lanchester of twenty years earlier) to have a chassis which was also part of its body. The chassis side members were extended upwards to form the sides. The aluminum skin was applied over this rigid skeleton. The engine and machinery were hung on an arrangement of tubes fastened to the enormously stiff structure.

TOP: *Pre-World War I Lancia Theta had quite conventional 5-litre, four-cylinder engine. Note its electric headlights and American-looking rumble seat. Bottom: Modern Lancia Flavia works its way through Milanese traffic.*

241

The story goes that Signor Lancia, out driving with his mother, broke a front leaf spring on a Kappa model and almost had a nasty accident. Charging back to his design department, he demanded a better kind of front suspension. The result was the unique system of vertical tubes which also acted as kingpins inside of which were coil springs. The tubes ended in little circular plates on the front fenders, and I remember dire but untrue tales about front springs flying out and making holes in people's foreheads if the plates were carelessly removed.

The Lambda's four-cylinder, single-overhead camshaft engine was one of the narrow, 20-degree, almost V's which were characteristic of Lancias for many years. (The modern six-cylinder Flaminia still is a V but with a 60-degree slope.) This engine had some oddities: its Zenith carburetor fed from the rear of the head through complex internal porting, and on early models (there were nine different series of Lambdas) the fan was whittled out of wood! Late Lambda engines developed about 65 hp at 3000 rpm from their 2359-cc engines.

*Lancia Aurelia which first appeared in 1950 with 1754-cc engine was pleasant, rather gutless 80-mph car.
But when 2½-litre Gran Turismo version appeared, Aurelia became one of the greatest Lancias ever. Aurelia B-20 would go from 0 to 60 in 12 seconds and exceed 105 mph. Fairly ugly two-seat convertible (top) is by Pininfarina.*

MIDDLE LEFT: *Aurelia sedan of 1957.*

MIDDLE RIGHT: *Current Fulvia Sport. Three of these 1290-cc front-drive Fulvias were among first five finishers in 1967 Monte Carlo Rally.*

BOTTOM: *Zagato-bodied Flaminia.*

Lambdas were surprisingly popular in this country. They cost only about $3,000 in the late twenties. I can remember as a small boy begging for catalogues in their 57th Street showroom in New York.

Since those days, Lancia has built cars of every size and type, all of the very first rank. Some were especially great: the posh V-8 Dilambda of 1928; the tiny, chassis-less Aprilia of 1936; and after World War II the wonderful Aurelia. I drove one of these quick, 2½-litre GT cars for a time and still consider it one of the most civilized machines ever.

For a time in the fifties, Gianni Lancia, Vincenzo's son (Vincenzo Lancia died in 1937 at fifty-six), embarked on a program of racing. Lancias won the Mille Miglia in 1954, the Mexican Carrera-Panamericana in 1953 (first, second, and third), and the Monte Carlo Rally in 1954.

In 1954 Lancia entered Grand Prix racing with a Formula I car designed in part by Vittoria Jano, the talented ex-Alfa Romeo engineer. Immediately, the new D-50 car made fastest lap time in the Spanish Grand Prix of 1954. The cars showed great promise, but the expensive G.P. program was too much of a strain for Lancia's finances and the cars were handed over to Ferrari.

Today Lancia still builds cars which are among the world's most desirable machines; the small 1290-cc front-drive Fulvia, capable of over 90 mph; the front-drive Flavia with a flat four, horizontally opposed, 1800-cc engine and a speed of over 115 mph; and the magnificent Flaminia, which in Zagato-bodied Supersport form can reach 130 mph with its V-6, 2775-cc engine.

In the 1967 Monte Carlo Rally, three out of the top five finishers were little 1290-cc Fulvia coupes. Lancias still are great cars.

ASTON

FLR 707

MARTIN

ASTON MARTIN I went riding some time ago in a late model Aston Martin. As we stopped for a red light near a shopping center, hairy youths assailed us with cries of "Gold-something-or-other!"

This unseemly recognition of what was once a car for the knowledgeable was, of course, the dismal result of press agentry. The use of a gilded Aston, dressed up with machine guns, tire slashers, a smoke screen, and what-not, for one of Mr. Ian Fleming's films may have helped sales, but to my mind it mostly gave the great old name of Aston Martin some low notoriety.

The $15,000 Aston Martin in which I rode, and briefly drove, was a very late one, a DB6. Like the Ferrari, the XK-E Jaguar, and the Lamborghini, it is a true GT car designed for the high speed, trans-Europe dashes in which ultrawealthy continental business bigwigs are said to indulge. And the cars are built to ensconce these people in all the padded luxury to which a flourishing European economy has accustomed them.

Climbing aboard I found myself almost smothered in the luxury of hand-sewn English leather, not only on the four seats (the two rear ones are minimal), but also on the door panels. The carpeting was deep and soft, the instrument panel was replete with sensible dials—including even an indicator for oil temperature—but the switchgear and other protuberances might receive demerits from our Mr. Nader.

On the road the DB6 feels just right. Almost vintage in its firmness, it still doesn't have that spine-jarring, rattle-provoking harshness of the old time pukka sports car. But it is harder than, say, a GT Ferrari. The firmness of the suspension is adjustable by means of a ride control, an unusual feature these days. The rack-and-pinion steering is beautifully accurate and gives one the feeling of actually having something to do with pointing the steering wheel.

Performance is what you might expect from 325 hp (at a mere 5750 rpm) hauling less than 4,000 pounds. I didn't time it myself, but 0 to 60 is on the order of 8 seconds. And a top speed around 140 is promised. The five-speed gearbox and the disc brakes made no impression on me at all. I suppose perfection becomes commonplace after you drive such a car for even a little while. The Aston's 4-litre engine, with its twin polished cam covers and triple Webers is, as ever, lovely to contemplate. The body design is unobtrusive, perhaps a little too unobtrusive. It's not exactly stodgy, but a road express like the Aston is a romantic car and should have coachwork that's right up there among the leaders, like Ferrari and Lamborghini.

The Aston Martin name goes back to 1913. Aston derived from the fact that its originators, Bamford and Martin, who were agents for Singer cars, sentimentally remembered the Aston-Clinton Hill on which they had competed in tuned Singers, and Martin after Lionel Martin, who had almost everything to do with the birth of the marque. It was Lionel Martin who, when he was dreaming of his ideal car, said that he wanted a machine which combined the qualities of a Bugatti and a Rolls-Royce. Their first Aston was really a 1908 racing Isotta-Fraschini with an L-head, 1389-cc Coventry-Simplex engine. It wasn't until after World War I that Aston Martin began building their own high-quality chassis.

But by 1926 only fifty cars had been sold and a new company, Aston Martin Motors Limited, was formed, which not only kept the name alive but soon started to build that most desirable series of Astons designed by

246

PRECEDING PAGES: *An Aston
Martin of the thirties was stark
and purposeful apparatus.
This is an Ulster of 1935. Similar
cars ran at Le Mans.*

TOP: *Team of 1½-litre Aston Martins used by factory for all racing in 1931, 1932, and 1933. They took first and second in 1931 Double Twelve, and one car, driven by Bertelli and Driscoll, won in 1932 Le Mans.*

MIDDLE LEFT: *Maurice Gatsonides was seventh in this DB2/4 Aston Martin in 1955 Monte Carlo Rally.*
MIDDLE RIGHT: *Tony Brooks in DBR1 that crashed at 1957 Le Mans.* ABOVE: *Brooks in Grand Prix Aston at Silverstone in 1959.*

Augustus Cesare Bertelli, who was the dominant force in the company. I still think that the Bertelli Aston Martins were just about the finest-looking sports cars of all time. Their angular radiators set well back behind the apron covering the big filler-capped oil tanks of their dry sump systems, multi-louvered hoods, helmeted cycle-type fenders, shining external exhaust pipes—all added up to a look calculated to make an enthusiast weak with yearning.

The first of these Bertelli Astons was the International, which was available to delighted private owners early in 1930. It had a 1½-litre engine with a single chain-driven overhead camshaft and Bertelli's unique "pent-roof" combustion chamber with the spark plug on top and both valves on one side. The four-speed, close-ratio gearbox was separated from the engine by a short shaft. Since the gearbox was well aft, it allowed the use of a short, stubby gear lever, thereby setting a fashion still with us. A torque tube and an underslung worm gear drove the rear wheels. Although one of Bertelli's pet components, it was the only part that usually gave trouble. An International was capable of about 80 mph.

In 1932, after Bertelli and co-driver Driscoll won the Biennal Cup at Le Mans, the Le Mans model came out. In 1933 the Mark II arrived. Now the engine delivered more power—about 75 hp. But the worm gear was dropped along with the torque tube. The separate gearbox was already gone.

Bertelli had by now lost full control. He had a joint managing director, R. Gordon Sutherland, whose father, Sir Arthur Sutherland, Bt., K.B.E., had come to the rescue of the financially ailing company.

Then came the potent 100-mph Ulster. But the Aston was changing with the times. It no longer had that old hand-fitted craftsmanship. More stampings rather than hand-filed castings were used. By 1936 the standard 15-98 Aston Martin had a 2-litre engine, no cycle fenders or dry sump lubrication. And, horrors, it had synchromesh gears. There was, however, a special 100-hp Speed Model that still retained the dry sump and a crash box.

Just before the war an experimental car with a prophetic name, the Atom, was built. With its integral body-chassis it foreshadowed the Astons of today. It had the standard 2-litre engine and a closed body, but during the war Claude Hill, its designer, continued working on a fast, open version. One of these driven by "Jock" Horsfall and Leslie Johnson won the Belgian twenty-four-hour race at Spa in 1948, and perhaps started Britain on its course toward the victories of today.

In 1947 David Brown, the gear and tractor man, bought Aston Martin and Lagonda. In 1950 the twin ohc 2.6 Lagonda engine designed by W. O. Bentley was installed in the Aston Martin and, voila!, new, lustier series of touring and highly successful racing DB Aston Martins were on their way.

LEFT *"Le Mans" model Aston Martin owned
by W. B. Fowler knocks over marker at Coronation
Rally. Extra set of headlights is
later addition. Half-hidden by rally marker
is filler for dry-sump oil tank.*

*Modern Aston Martin is
one of the world's great Gran Turismo machines.
Below is DB5 with svelte Italian
body by Zagato, and, at bottom, current DB6
with now-fashionable spoiler tail.*

Picture Credits

TB—Tom Burnside
RM—Rupert Mountain Automotive Research
LI—Long Island Auto Museum, Albert Mecham Collection
DP—Detroit Public Library, Automotive History Collection
JW—Julius Weitmann
(Names in parentheses refer to car owners.)

WHAT MADE THEM GREAT: 6-7 LI. 11 RM. 12 (top) "Old Motor," London; (bottom) RM. 14-15 (upper left) White Motor Co.; (others) LI. 17 Original poster painting from Alec Riemer Auto Museum, Drieghbergen, Holland. 19 LI.

INVICTA: 20-21 TB (Vojta Mashek). 23 TB. 25 (top) RM; (bottom left and right) TB.

TALBOT-LAGO: 26-27 TB (Vojta Mashek). 28 TB. 31 TB. 32-33 (left) Ralph Stein Collection; (right) RM.

LANCHESTER: 34-35 TB (Francis W. Hutton-Stott). 37 TB. 38 (top left) Science Museum, London; (top right and bottom) RM. 39 (top left) RM; (top right) TB; (bottom) Francis W. Hutton-Stott. 40 TB. 41 Francis W. Hutton-Stott. 42 RM.

HISPANO-SUIZA: 44-45 TB (Nicholas Franco, Jr.). 46 RM. 49 (top) RM; (bottom left and right) RM, Wallace C. Bird Collection. 50-51 (left) TB (Richard E. Riegel, Jr.); (right, top two) TB (Richard E. Riegel, Jr.); (bottom three) TB (Peter Hampton). 52 TB.

ALFA ROMEO: 54-55 TB (George W. Huguely). 58 TB. 60 RM. 62 & 65 Alfa Romeo, Italy. 66 (top left and bottom) Alfa Romeo; (top right) Ralph Stein Collection. 67 TB (Vojta Mashek). 68-69 (top and bottom) Alfa Romeo; (middle) TB.

VAUXHALL: 70-71 TB (Ken Ball). 72 Vauxhall Motors. 75 TB (Vauxhall Motors) 76-77 (top left) TB; (middle left) Ralph Stein Collection; (lower left and right) Vauxhall Motors.

ROLLS-ROYCE: 78-79 TB (Harrah's Automobile Collection, Reno, Nevada). 80-81 RM. 83 TB. 85 TB (F. M. Wilcock). 86-87 RM. 88 (top) TB (Ann Klein); (bottom) TB (Melanie Monroe). 93 TB (Vincent Sardi, Jr.). 94 (top two and bottom) RM; (middle) TB.

BENTLEY: 96 TB (Ann Klein). 98-99 TB (Ann Klein). 102 (top) TB; (bottom) Ralph Stein Collection. 103 TB (Ann Klein). 104 TB (Bill Lake). 105 RM.

DUESENBERG: 106-107 TB (George W. Huguely). 109 DP. 110-111 TB (top) (Harrah's Automobile Collection, Reno, Nevada), (bottom right) (Richard E. Riegel, Jr.). 112 (top and bottom right) RM; (lower left) TB.

FRAZER NASH: 114-115 TB (George Schieffelin). 116 RM. 118-119-121 TB.

CORD: 122-123 TB (Harrah's Automobile Collection, Reno, Nevada). 124 TB (Richard Devin). 126-127 (left top and bottom) TB; (right) RM.

MERCEDES-BENZ: 128-129 TB (Peter Hampton). 131 "Old Motor," London. 132 TB (top) (Francis W. Hutton-Stott), (middle) (Vojta Mashek), (bottom) (Peter Hampton). 134 (top and middle) "Old Motor," London; (bottom two) TB. 136-138 RM. 141 TB.

FERRARI: 142-143 TB (Julius Weitmann). 145 (top) Pininfarina; (lower left) Irv Dolin; (lower right) JW. 147 JW. 149 TB (George W. Huguely).

SIMPLEX: 150 RM. 152-153 (top two) TB; (top right) Harrah's Automobile Collection, Reno, Nevada; (bottom two) RM. 154 RM. 155 DP. 157 TB (Ed Roy).

BUGATTI: 158-159 TB (Peter Hampton). 162-163 (top and bottom right) TB (Dr. Peter Williamson); (bottom left) RM. 164 (top two) TB (Vojta Mashek); (bottom) "Autocar," England. 166-167 TB (Harrah's Automobile Collection, Reno, Nevada). 168 TB (Peter Hampton). 171 TB (George W. Huguely). 172-173 TB (top right) (Harrah's Automobile Collection, Reno, Nevada), (bottom right) (Peter Hampton). 174 (top and bottom) TB (Harrah's Automobile Collection, Reno, Nevada); (middle) Ralph Stein Collection. 175 "Autocar," England.

MERCER: 176-177 TB (Edward King). 178 TB (Harrah's Automobile Collection, Reno, Nevada). 180 TB (Jerry Foley). 183 (top) Ralph Buckley; (bottom) LI.

M.G.: 184-185 TB (C. N. Coles). 186 RM. 188 M.G. Car Co. 189 TB (M.G. Car Co.). 190 M.G. Car Co. 192-193 TB (M.G. Car Co.). 195 M.G. Car Co.

JAGUAR: 196-197 TB (Vojta Mashek). 199 TB. 200 (top) Bill Large; (bottom) RM. 201 (top) TB; (bottom) RM. 204-205 Jaguar Car Co.

STUTZ: 206-207 TB (Harrah's Automobile Collection, Reno, Nevada). 209 Rockefeller Museum, Arkansas. 210 TB (top two) (Harrah's Automobile Collection, Reno, Nevada).

DELAGE: 212-213 RM. 214-215 TB (top left & right) (André Surmain); (bottom left & right) (Vojta Mashek). 217 JW. 218-219 (top and bottom right) RM; (middle and bottom left) DP.

LINCOLN: 220-221 TB (Joe Josephs). 223 (top two) TB (Andrew Hotton); (bottom) RM.

ISOTTA-FRASCHINI: 224-225 DP, Lazarnick Collection. 227 RM. 229 (top, lower left and middle) TB; (lower right) Ralph Stein Collection.

PACKARD: 231 RM. 232-233-234-235 TB. 236-237 TB (Harrah's Automobile Collection, Reno, Nevada).

LANCIA: 238-239 RM. 240-241 TB. 242-243 RM.

ASTON MARTIN: 244-245 TB (Al Scully). 247 (middle right) JW; (others) RM. 248-249 (top left and right) RM; (lower right) TB.

Index

Numbers in italics refer to illustrations.

Aldington, H.J. and W.H., 116, 120
Alfa Romeo, 47, 56-68, *162*
  2.3, *54-55, 58, 62,* 64,
    65, 67
  2.6, 64
  1500 cc, 59, *62*
  1750 cc, 59, 61-64, *62,* 194, 230
  2900B, *65, 66,* 68
  Corto, 68
  Duetto, 68, *68-69*
  Giulia, 68, *69*
  Giulietta, *69*
  Gran Sport, 61, *66*
  Lungo, 68
  P2, 56, 59, *62*
  RL series, 57
  RLSS 22/90, 56-59
  Spyder, *69*
  Super Sport, 61, *66*
  TF series, 59
Alfonso XIII, King, 53
Amilcar, 187
Arkus-Duntov, Zora, 30, *32*
Ascari, Alberto, *142-43*
Ascari, Antonio, 59, 146
Aston Martin, 195, 198, 202, 246-48
  1½-litre, *247*
  DB series, 246, *247,* 248, *249*
  International, 248
  Le Mans, *248,* 248
  Mark II, 248
  Ulster, *244-45,* 248
Auburn, 113, 125, 127
Austin, *199,* 202
Austin Healey Sprite, 195
Austro-Daimler, 137
Auto-Union, 29, 64, 137, 148, 169

Baker, "Cannonball," 209
Baracca, Francesco, 148
Barbarou, Marius, 137
Barnato, Woolf, 48, 101, 105, 211
Bauer, Wilhelm, 130
Becchia, Walter, 29
Bentley, 97-105
  1967 model, *105*
  3-litre, 97, *102, 103, 104*
  4-litre, *94, 98-99,* 101
  4½-litre, 24, *96,* 100, 101, *104*
  6½-litre, 100, 101
  8-litre, *103,* 105
  Big Six, 100
  Green Label, 97
  Mark V, 95
  Mark VI, 95
  Red Label, 97
  Speed Six, 100, *104*
Bentley, Walter Owen, 53, 92, 97, 100,
    101, *105,* 211, 248
Benz, *12, 131,* 135, 137
  Blitzen, 137
  Parsifal, 137
Benz, Carl, 36, 130, 135
Bertelli, Augustus Cesare, 248
Birkigt, Mark, 9, 48, 53
Birkin, Sir Henry (Tim), 24, 64, 101
B.M.W., 120
Bond, Ed, 64
Broesel, Herman, 155
Brooks, Tony, *247*
Brown, David, 248
Buckley, Ralph, 151, 156, *227*
Buehrig, Gordon, 113, 127
Bugatti, 56, 160-75
  "Black Bess," *158-59*
  Brescia, 165, 169
  Brescia Modifié, *165,* 169
  Type 30, *168*
  Type 35, *162-63, 164,* 165

Type 37, *164*
Type 40, 160
Type 41 Royale (Golden Bug), 108,
    170, *174*
Type 43, 56, 160, 169
Type 46, 170
Type 49, 170
Type 50, *166-67*
Type 51, 161, *162,* 169
Type 54, 169
Type 55, 144, 161-65, *173*
Type 57, 56, 161, 170, *171, 172,*
    173, 174, 203
Type 59, 169, *175*
Type 64, 170
Type 68, 175
Type 73, 175
Type 101, *174,* 175
Bugatti, Ettore, 9, 56, 160, 165, 170,
    175, 226, 230
Burman, Bob, 137

Cadillac, 211, 237
Campari, *62*
Campbell, Malcolm, 63
Caters, Baron de, 135
Caracciola, Rudolf, 139, 140-41
Chevrolet, 113
Clark, Henry Austin, Jr., 156, *183,*
    226, 236
Collier, Barron, Jr., 187
Collier, Miles, 187, 191, 194
Collier, Sam, 187
Colombo, Gioacchino, 146
Comotti, Gianfranco, 29
Cord, 57, 125-27
  L 29, *127,* 127
  Model 810, 125, *126,* 127, 216
  Model 812, 122-23, *124,* 125, *126*
Cord, Erret Lobban, 113, 127
Corderey, Violet, 22
Corvette, 30, 202, 211
Coventry Climax, 203
Crane-Simplex, 47, 156
Croker, Frank, 156
Cuccio, John, 144-46

Daimler, *12,* 43, 87, 130, 203
Daimler, Gottlieb, 36, 130
Daimler, Paul, 130
Daimler-Phoenix-Wagen, 130, *132*
Decauville, 88
De Dion, *17,* 235
De Dion quadricycle, 88
Delage, 216-19
  4-litre, 219
  6¼-litre, 217
  10.7-litre, 217
  D6-70, *218,* 219
  D8 series, *212-13, 214,* 219
  D8/120, *214, 215,* 216, 219
  DIS, 219
  DISS, 219
  Grand Prix, 217-19, *217, 218*
Delage, Louis, 217, 219
Delahaye, 22, 198, 219
Delling, Erik H., 182
DePalma, Ralph, 182
D.F.P., 100
Dinsmore, Clarence Gray, 135
Dreyfus, René, 29
Dubonnet, André, 47, 48
Duesenberg, 57, 108-13, 125, 127
  A model, 113
  J model, *106-7,* 108, *112,* 113
  SJ model, *110-11, 112,* 113
Duesenberg, August, 113
Duesenberg, Fred, 108, 113
Durant, William Crapo, 222

Duray, Leon, 169
Dymaxion Transport, 29

Elcar, 182
Enever, Syd, 195
Erle, Fritz, 137
Eyston, George, 95

Fane, A.F.P., *116,* 120
Fantacci, Giuseppe, 59-61
Ferrari, 30, 68, 144-48, 202, 219,
    243, 246
  2½-litre Grand Prix, *142-43*
  275 GTB4, 146, *148*
  330 GTC 2+2, 146
  365/P Berlinetta Speciale, 146
  375 Mille Miglia, *145*
  Berlinetta, 144
  Spyder GTS, 146
  Super America, *148*
  Type 125, *145,* 146
Ferrari, Enzo, 9, 146
Fetch, Tom, 235
F.I.A.T., 241
Ford, 146, 160, 216, 222
Ford, Edsel, 222
Ford, Henry, 36, 222
Franklin, 13
Franquist, Edward, 155
Fraschini, Oreste, 227
Frazer Nash, 117-20
  Blackburne-engined, *114-15, 118,* 119
  Le Mans Replica, *121*
  sporting model, *116*
Frazer-Nash, Archie, 120
Fuller, Buckminster, 29

Gerard, Louis, 219
Gilhooley, Ray, 74
Glidden, J.S., *14*
G.N., 120
Godfrey, H. R., 120
Grier, Robert S., 30, 216
Griswold, Frank, 68
Guynemer, Georges, 47

Hall, E. R., 92
Halley, Maclure, 29, 68, 230
Hamilton, Duncan, *200*
Hancock, A. J., *72*
Hare, Emlen S. 156, 182
Harmsworth, Sir Alfred, 9
Hawthorne, Mike, *145*
Healey, Donald, 24
Héméry, Victor, 137
Hill, Claude, 248
Hill, Phil, *147*
Hispano-Suiza, 9, 47-53
  1910 racing car, *46*
  3-litre, 53
  5-litre, 53
  Alfonso XIII, *44-45, 52,* 53
  Boulogne, 48, *50, 51, 52*
  H6 37.2, 47, *49,* 97
  Pegaso, 53
  Type 68, *51,* 53
Horsfall, "Jock," 248
Howe, Lord, 64, 95

Invicta, 22-25
  1½-litre, 24
  Black Prince, 25
  S-type, *20-21,* 22, *23, 25,* 216
  Sports, 22
Isotta, Cesare, 227
Isotta-Fraschini, 90, 108, 226-28, 246
  IM series, 226, *229*
  KM series, 226, *227*
  Monterosa, 228

Tipo 8 series, 228, *229*
Voiturette, *224-25*, 226

Jaguar, 61, 195, 198-203
  420G Grand Saloon, *205*
  C type, *201*
  D type, *200*
  Mark II, *205*
  Mark IV, 203
  Mark V, 203
  SS series, *196-97, 199,* 202-03
  XK-E, 198, 202, 203, *204*, 246
  XK-SS, 203, *204*
  XK-120, *200, 202,* 203
  XK-150, *205*
Jano, Vittorio, 59, 64, 68, 243
Jellinek, Emile, 130, 133
Jenatzy, Camille, *134*, 135
Johnson, Leslie, 248

Kettering, C.F., 48
Kimber, Cecil, *186*, 187, 191

Lace, A.C., 24
Lago, Antony, 29-30, 33
Lamborghini, 246
Lanchester, 36-43, 241
  1897 model, *38*
  1900 model, *38*
  1901 model, 36
  1903 model, *39*
  1905 model, 43
  1912 model, *41*
  1913 Torpedo Tourer, *34-35, 37*
  1914 Sporting Forty, *42*
  1930 model, 42
Lanchester, Frederick, 36, 40, 41, 43
Lanchester, George, 36, 43
Lanchester, Nancy, *42*
Lancia, 241-43
  Aprilia, 243
  Aurelia, *242,* 243
  Dilambda, 243
  D-50 Grand Prix, 243
  Flaminia, *242,* 243
  Flàvia, *240,* 243
  Fulvia, *242,* 243
  Kappa, 243
  Lambda, *238-39,* 241-43
  Theta, *240*
Lancia, Gianni, 243
Lancia, Vincenzo, 241, 243
Lebegue, René, 29, 30
Leland, Henry M., 36, 222
Levegh, Pierre, 30
Lincoln, 57, 90, 211, 222-23
  1920 model, 222
  Continental, 223
  KA V-12, 223
  KB, 220-21, 222, *223,* 223
  Leland, *223*
  Model K, 222
  Zephyr, 223
Lockhart, Frank, 211
Lory, M., 219
Lotus, 113
Lycett, Forrest, 105
Lyons, William, 202

Macklin, Noël, 22
Maeder, Werner, 30, 216
Martin, Lionel, 246
Maserati, 30, 146, *162*
Maybach, Wilhelm, 130
Mays, Raymond, 24, 120, 169
Mercedes, 16, 130-35
  1904 racing car, *134*
  1905 racing car, *134*
  1921 28/95, *136*
  American-built, 135
  Sixty, *132,* 133-35, *134,* 141
  Ninety, 135
Mercedes-Benz, 29, 30, 63-64,
  130-41, 146, 148

230 SL, *141,* 141
300 SL, *138,* 141
540K, 24, *132,* 141
600, *141*
K (33/180), *136,* 139
S series, *128-29,* 139, 141
SS series, 140, 141
SSK series, *138,* 140, 141
SSKL series, *138,* 140, 141
Mercer, 179-82, 209
  Elcar, 182
  Raceabout, 53, *176-77, 178,* 179-81,
    180, 182, *183,* 209
  Speedster, *178,* 181
M.G., 120, 187-95
  C types, *188,* 191
  J types, *184-85,* 187, *188, 190*
  K3 Magnette, 187, *192*
  M types, 187, *188, 189*
  MGA, 195
  MGB, *195,* 195
  Mark III Tigress, *186*
  Midget, 187, *188,* 191
  Old Number One, *186*
  P types, 191
  Q types, 191
  R types, 191
  T types, *190,* 191-95, *193*
Molsheim Buick, 170
Morris, William, 187
Moscovics, Frederic E., 209
Murphy, Jimmy, 113

Nance, Jim, 237
Napier-Bentley, 105
Nibel, Hans, 137, 140
Nuvolari, Tazio, *65*

Oldfield, Barney, 137, 182
Oliver, Smith Hempstone, 208

Packard, 57, 90, 211, 230-37
  120, 237
  1906 model, *231*
  1910 model, *234*
  1934 V-12, *237*
  Clipper, 237
  Golden Anniversary, 237
  "Gray Wolf," 235
  Light Eight, 237
  Model F, *236*
  "Old Pacific," 235
  Speedster, 230, *235*
  Thirty, *232-33, 234,* 236
  Twin-Six, 236
Packard, James Ward, 234-35
Paget, Dorothy, 101
Panhard-Levassor, *12,* 36, 87, 88, *133*
Panzer Kraft-Wagonen, 137-39
Peerless, *19*
Peugeot, *12*
Pomeroy, Laurence, Jr., 73, *76*
Pomeroy, Laurence, Sr., *12,* 74
Porsche, 195
Porsche, Ferdinand, 137-39, 140
Porter, Finley Robertson, 179, 182, *183*
Post, Augustus, *14*
Pullen, Eddie, 182

Rand, George, *145*
Renault, 139
Rickenbacker, Eddie, *109*
Roebling family, 181, 182
Roger-Benz, 135
Rolls, Charles S., *80,* 88
Rolls-Bentley, 24, 92
Rolls-Royce, 13, 81-95, 108, 223, 227, 228
  20/25, 92
  25/30, *88,* 92
  30 hp, *80*
  "Baby" (20 hp), 92
  Bentley, 24, 92, *94,* 95
  Legalimit, 90
  Light Twenty, *80*

Phantom I, 90-92, *94,* 101
Phantom II, 91-95, 230
Phantom III, *93,* 95
Silver Cloud, 95
Silver Dawn, 95
Silver Ghost, 47, *78-79,* 81-87, *83, 85,*
  86-87, 88, 89, 90
Silver Shadow, 47, *94,* 95
Silver Wraith, 92, 95
Two-cylinder, *80,* 89

Rosier, Louis, 30
Roy, Ed, *217,* 217
Royce, Frederick Henry, 53, 81, 82, 87,
  88, 95, 160
Rubin, Bernard, 101

Schwab, Charles M., 209
Seaman, Richard, 219
Segrave, Henry, 169
Simca, 33
Simplex, 151-56
  1904 racing car, *154*
  1905 model, *154*
  1906 model, *153*
  50-hp, 151, *152, 153,* 156, *157*
  75-hp, 156
  90-hp, 151, 156
  Zip racing car, *155*
Singer, 187, 246
Sivocci, Ugo, 59, 146
Snyder, William P., 111, 226, *227*
Spence, Bill, *112*
Standard, 202
Studebaker, 216
Stutz, 208-11
  American Underslung, 208
  Bearcat, 179, *206, 207,* 208-09
  Bearcat Torpedo Speedster, 211
  Black Hawk, 48, *210,* 211
  Bulldog, 209
  D.V. 32, *210,* 211
  Pak-Age-Car, 211
  Safety, 209-11
  Super Bearcat, *209,* 211
Stutz, Harry C., 208, 209
Sutherland, Sir Arthur, 248
Swallow Side Car and Coach Building
  Company, 202
Swift, 202

Talbot-Darracq, 29, 33
Talbot-Lago, 29-33
  4½-liter, 29, 30, *31, 32*
  America, 33
  Baby, 33
  Grand Sport, 30
  Record, 33
  Type 150-SS, *26-27, 28,* 29, *31*
Templar, Guy, 24
Thomas, E. R., 90
Thomas, René, 217
Toronado, 125
Triumph, 195

Ulmann, Alec, 97

Varzi, Achille, 169
Vauxhall, 73-77
  1909 model, *75*
  1914 racing car, *72,* 77
  O.E. 30-98, 73, 74, *75, 76,* 77
  Prince Henry, *12, 70-71,* 73, 74, *76*
Volkswagen, 137

Welch, 13, 90, 226
White Steamer, *14, 15*
Winton, Alexander, 234-35
Wolseley, 202

Young, A. B. Filson, 133

Zucarelli, Paul, *46,* 53
Zumbach's, 24, 30, 59